Cycling Canada

Cycling
Canada

Bicycle Touring Adventures in Canada

John M. Smith

Bicycle Books – San Francisco

Published by:
Bicycle Books, Inc.
1282 - 7th Avenue
San Francisco, CA 94122
U.S.A.

Distributed to the book trade by:
U.S.A. National Book Network, Lanham, MD
Canada Raincoast Book Distribution
U.K. Chris Lloyd Sales and Marketing Services, Poole, Dorset

Cover design by Kent Lytle, Lytle Design, Alameda
Cover photograph courtesy Alberta Tourism, taken at Bow Lake,
Banff National Park

Credit has been given for submitted photos;
uncredited photos are those of the author.

Cataloging in Publication Data
Smith, John M. 1945–
Cycling Canada: Bicycle Touring Adventures in Canada
Series title: The Active Travel Series
Bibliography: p. Includes index
1. Bicycles and bicycling, touring guides
2. Travel, Canada
I. Title
II. Authorship

Library of Congress Catalog Card No. 95-76301
ISBN 0-933201-70-2 Paperback original

Acknowledgements

A great number of people have helped to make this book a reality, and I would like to thank them all. Our love of cycling has resulted in *Cycling Canada*, intended as a reference and help to other cyclists.

In particular, I would like to thank the various provincial cycling associations and the provincial tourist offices that have been so helpful in accumulating the data for this book. I would also like to thank the contributors of important tour details for their additions.

I would like to thank those who helped in the preparation of the maps and photos.

I would like to thank the sports and photography departments of my local newspaper, the *Intelligencer*, for their assistance.

I would like to thank my publisher for believing in this book.

And I would like to thank my wife, Marion, and our family for helping me to write—and to live—this book.

About the Author

John M. Smith is a graduate of Wilfrid Laurier University, Waterloo, Ontario. He lives in Prince Edward County and teaches English in Belleville. He has not only toured through all the provinces and territories of Canada, but has also done extensive touring in the United States, Asia, Mexico, Europe, New Zealand, and Australia. This is his first book, but he has written extensively for various magazines.

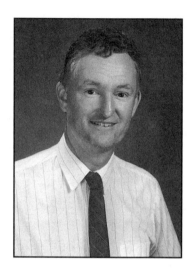

Table of Contents

Chapter 1

Bicycle Touring in Canada

Canada is one of the best places for bicycle touring, certainly in the Western Hemisphere. Once you accept that the daunting size of the country (far bigger than the United States, not to mention England) should not force you to cover the entire country in one trip, you can get down to selecting a suitable region and experiencing some of the finest scenery and some of the best roads and infrastructure anywhere in the world.

Getting to Canada

From the U.S. and other countries, Canada is easily accessible by train, plane, boat, and motor vehicle. Boats dock at many of the large ports in Canada. Rail service is available across mainland Canada, from British Columbia to Nova Scotia. Bus service is readily available in all ten provinces and the Territories. International airports are located at both sides of

Cyclists checking out their route. (Photo courtesy New Brunswick Tourism)

this vast country (Vancouver and Victoria in British Columbia; Gander and St. John's in Newfoundland) and at many centers in between; for more information, contact:

Air Canada by phoning (514) 393-3333 or 1-800-422-6232

Canadian Airlines International by phoning 1-800-426-7000.

If you are planning on cycling a long distance, it is generally better to plan a west-to-east route (as you are more likely to get an assisting breeze at your back).

Transporting Your Bicycle

If transporting your bicycle by plane or train, be prepared to disassemble and pack your bicycle in a box. Boxes may be available at the airport or station, but you can get one in advance from a bicycle shop. (For a price, they'll even pack it properly for you.) Some airlines make you sign a waiver form to indicate that they are not responsible for any damage to your bike (your house insurance should cover your bicycle).

Some airlines allow a bicycle as your first piece of luggage; others consider it excess baggage and charge a flat fee for the bike, so it's best to ask the airline. For example, both Air Canada and Canadian Airlines International will require the bicycle to be boxed or bagged, with handlebars sideways and pedals removed; there will be no additional charge for the bicycle on international flights, if it is considered one of the allowed two pieces of luggage.

American Residents Visiting Canada

Passports are not required of U.S. citizens; however, you must carry proof of citizenship, such as a birth certificate. Proof of residence may be required. Minors (under 18) traveling without parent or guardian must also carry a notarized letter of consent. Naturalized citizens should have naturalization papers. Resident aliens must have an Alien Registration Card.

If you are planning to drive in Canada, you must have a Canadian Non-Resident Inter-Provincial Motor Vehicle Liability Insurance Card; this card is proof of financial responsibility. Vehicle registration cards are needed. If you are driving someone else's vehicle into Canada, you must have written permission from the owner (or a copy of the rental agreement for a rental vehicle).

Passports and Visas

Visitors entering Canada from countries other than the United States must have valid national passports or acceptable travel documents and, in some cases, entry visas. A list of countries from which a visa is required for entry into Canada is available from Employment and Immigration Canada.

Maps and Information

If you want maps of particular provinces or areas in Canada, you can receive them free of charge from the provincial tourist offices. These offices will gladly send you information about the areas, too (the addresses and phone numbers are given in Chapters 4–14, where specific recommended trips are described).

The Law

In the following sections, we will examine some of the legal aspects as they apply to cycle tourists visiting Canada. Of course, except for the rules concerning entry into the country, these same laws apply equally to Canadian residents.

Entry to Canada

Tourists with convictions (felony convictions, driving while intoxicated convictions, etc.) may be denied admittance into Canada. For information, contact:

Canada Customs
Communications Branch
Ottawa, Ontario K1A 0L5
Telephone (613) 957-0275

Driving in Canada

Legal minimum driving ages vary from province to province. Seat belts must be worn.

Littering

Littering is an offence in Canada. The fines vary from province to province. Leave Canada as clean as you find it.

Alcoholic Beverages

The legal age for the consumption of alcoholic beverages is 19 (18 in Quebec).

Fishing and Hunting Regulations

Fishing licenses are required.

Firearms are regulated by classification. All firearms must be declared upon entering the country. Firearm laws vary by province. Contact the following address:

Revenue Canada
Customs and Excise
Inspection and Control Division
Connaught Bldg.
Mackenzie Ave.
Ottawa, Ontario K1A 0L5
Telephone (613) 954-7142

Hunting and Fishing Guides are available from tourism outlets listed in Chapters 4–14.

Cycling Laws

When sharing the road, always cycle with the traffic and obey the rules of the road (in Canada, this includes cycling on the right-hand side of the road). All bicycles must be equipped with an adequate horn or bell and, if riding at night, you must have a light.

Chapter 2

About Canada

Dealing with the Climate

You have probably heard about the severe snowstorms that at times plague parts of Canada. However, Canadian summers are relatively mild and pleasant. Even the winters are not all that bad but it is tough pedaling through snow.

Average summer temperatures have been given for each province (in Chapters 4–14, where the recommended trips are described). In general, though, it is safe to cycle anywhere in Canada during the summer months. Yes, you could hit a sudden snowstorm in the mountains in July, as I have, but this is not the norm.

It is best to dress in layers and be prepared for changes in the weather. The greatest variety of temperatures are found in the western and northern mountains. There is a very noticeable change from a mountain valley to a summit. In general, be prepared for cooler temperatures at mountain

Spring weather in the valleys, and winter on the mountains just miles away. Revelstoke, British Columbia.

summits and in coastal areas, as opposed to central Canada, where prairie summers are usually dry and warm. Certain regions of Canada, particularly the coastal areas, receive a fair amount of rain, so be prepared with proper rain gear.

The spectacle of the changing colors of the leaves makes the early autumn another enticing time to cycle in parts of Canada.

Geography

If you are looking to cycle on peaceful islands, away from the crowds, try exploring Canada's coastal areas.

If you wish to cycle in some of the most spectacular mountain scenery anywhere in the world, ride in the Rocky Mountains of British Columbia and Alberta.

If you prefer quiet, rural settings, visit the Qu'Appelle Valley in Saskatchewan, Prince Edward County or Manitoulin Island in Ontario, or the Magdalen Islands of Quebec.

If you prefer to cycle on designated bicycle paths, away from road traffic, visit Kananaskis Country in Alberta, the Thousand Islands Bikeway or the Niagara Falls Recreational Trail in Ontario, or Prince Edward Island National Park on Prince Edward Island.

If your preference is for an adventurous wilderness experience, try cycling in Gros Morne National Park in Newfoundland or on the Dempster Highway in Canada's northern Territories. Simply put, Canada has a great variety of terrain and opportunity for the cyclist. British Columbia's island-dotted coast and the western mountains give way to the central prairies and wheatfields. The ruggedness of the Canadian Shield and the Laurentian Plateau give way to the red soil and relative flatness of the east coast's Prince Edward Island. In turn, this terrain is replaced by the rugged, rocky landscape of Canada's easternmost province, Newfoundland.

Wildlife

With the diversity of Canada's terrain, there is also a tremendous variety of wildlife. Particular species of wildlife that you might see have been given in the descriptions of some of the specific recommended tours, but Canada's wildlife includes numerous species, ranging from the hummingird to the elk to the mountain goat.

There is little to fear from the wildlife, but precautions must be taken not to frighten a potentially dangerous animal (such as a bear). Two rules apply:

1. Do make noise. If the animal hears and smells you, it will probably just wander away.

2. Do not feed wild animals or come between a mother and her baby.

History of Canada

As an independent nation, Canada is relatively young, yet some areas of the country have been inhabited for thousands of years.

In 1534, Jacques Cartier landed on what is now Canada (Quebec; Prince Edward Island) and claimed the territory for France. As time passed, there was a French-British struggle for supremacy. By 1840, Lower Canada (Quebec) and Upper Canada (Ontario) were joined (the Act of Union), and a stable, responsible government was instituted. Both joined the Canadian confederation of provinces in 1867.

Reference map for the provinces.

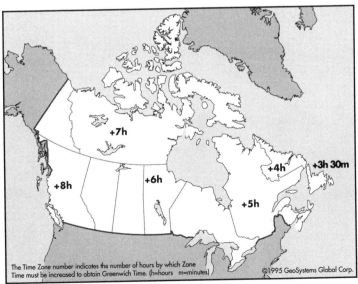

The Time Zone number indicates the number of hours by which Zone Time must be increased to obtain Greenwich Time. (h=hours   m=minutes)   ©1995 GeoSystems Global Corp.

One of the most important events in Canadian history was the creation of the Dominion of Canada on July 1, 1867. Since then, Canada has grown to consist of 10 provinces and the northern Territories. Newfoundland (including part of Labrador) was the last province to join Canada, on March 31, 1949.

The elected leader of Canada is called the Prime Minister. The Houses of Parliament are situated in Canada's capital, Ottawa, Ontario.

Metric Conversion

Canada operates on the metric system of measurement, as does most of the world. If you are not familiar with it, use the following guidelines.

Distance:

1 kilometer (km) = 0.6 mile
1 mi. = 1.6 km

Temperature:

Celsius to Fahrenheit
$F = (9/5 \times C) + 32$
For example,
$20°C = (9/5 \times 20) + 32 = 68°F$

Fahrenheit to Celsius
$C = 5/9 \times (F - 32)$
For example,
$77°F = 5/9 \times (77 - 32) = 25°C$

Weights, sizes, volumes:

1 kilogram (kg) = 2.2 lbs.
1 lb. = 0.45 kg
1 liter (l) = 1.8 pints
4.5 l = 1 Imperial gallon
3.8 l = 1 U.S. gallon
1 meter = 3.28 feet

1 foot = 0.3 meter
1 meter = 1.09 yards
1 yard = 0.91 meter
1 inch = 2.54 centimeters (cm)
1 cm = 0.39 inch

Money Matters

Visitors to Canada from abroad are encouraged to exchange funds for Canadian dollars at a bank or foreign currency exchange outlet to receive the prevailing rate of exchange.

The Canadian dollar is weak at the time this book goes to press, which is good news for visitors.

Canada has a provincial sales tax, which varies from province to province. In addition, there is a Goods and Services Tax (GST); however, non-Canadians may apply for a GST rebate on many items, including short-term accommodations (but not restaurant charges). Brochures explaining the GST and containing a rebate form are available at customs offices, duty-free shops, and tourist information centers. For more information, write:

Revenue Canada
Customs and Excise
Visitors' Rebate Program
Ottawa, Ontario K1A 1J

You may also obtain information by phoning 1-800 668-4748 (in Canada) and (613) 991-3346 (outside of Canada).

It is not advisable to carry large amounts of cash with you. If you do, be aware that some banks will not accept large denominations of foreign currency for exchange. Also, many Canadian businesses will not accept personal checks. It is, therefore, best to bring travelers' checks with you or use your credit cards to purchase most items.

Many of Canada's ATMs are part of a network that enables U.S. visitors to withdraw Canadian funds from the machine.

Banking hours vary by branch, but they are generally open from at least 10 A.M. to 4 P.M.; many have prolonged hours of operation.

Health, Water, and Food

Visitors from other countries are advised to obtain or extend health insurance coverage before departing for Canada. If you are taking a prescription drug, bring a copy of the prescription with you, in case a Canadian doctor needs to renew it for you.

Although Canada has a great supply of fresh water, contaminants are found in many of the lakes and rivers; therefore, it is advisable to boil any water taken from lakes or streams. Fill your water bottle(s) at restaurants, etc. (yes, you can drink the water).

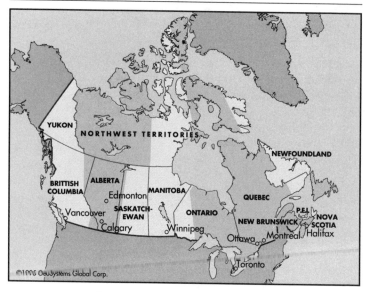

Time zones in Canada.

Canada is fortunate to have stringent food services restrictions; you can eat with confidence in the great variety of food-service establishments that you will encounter on your cycling trip.

Time Zones

Canada has 6 time zones.

When it's 7 P.M. in most of British Columbia (Pacific Standard Time), it's 8 P.M. in Alberta, northeastern British Columbia, and part of Saskatchewan (Mountain Standard Time), 9 P.M. in Manitoba, southeastern Saskatchewan, and northwestern Ontario (Central Standard Time), 10 P.M. in most of Ontario and Quebec (Eastern Standard Time), 11 PM in Nova Scotia, New Brunswick, Prince Edward Island, and part of Quebec (Atlantic Standard Time), and 11:30 PM in Newfoundland and Labrador (Newfoundland Standard Time).

Chapter 3

Pre-Trip Planning

Part of the exhilaration of bicycle touring—whether in Canada or elsewhere—is the independence you derive from traveling with just a bicycle and what you are carrying; it is, therefore, very important to buy wisely to ensure a safe and comfortable journey.

This book should prove very valuable to the independent cyclist. If you enjoy traveling alone, as I do, this book can help you organize your itinerary; however, it is hoped that there will always be a flexibility to your traveling plans.

Groups can also plan their own independent tours with the help of this book. Many cyclists prefer the camaraderie and organized aspects of a planned trip. Many bicycle touring companies are available (a list of many of them appears in the Appendix). The Appendix also lists addresses and phone numbers that provide other ways to obtain information.

Using this Book

In Chapters 4–15, over 100 specific bicycle trips are described, arranged by province, as well as a transcontinental crossing route with alternative options. Each chapter starts off with general information about the province, followed by descriptions of the individual routes.

Each tour description includes:

☐ The distance of the trip (in km and miles)

☐ The suggested number of days for that tour

☐ The difficulty of the tour:
   Easy (quite level)
   Moderate (some hilly or challenging sections)
   Strenuous (very challenging)

☐ The type of tour:
   Loop route (you end up where you started)
   Return trip (you return along the same route)
   One-way tour

☐ Information on getting to your starting point, and back from your destination.

☐ Accommodations information for that route

☐ References for getting more information (phone numbers and addresses for cycling information, tourist information, maps, etc.)

☐ A map of the route

☐ A description of the specific route, with points of interest

☐ Optional cycling routes

☐ Optional things to do on the route

Your Bicycle

The best bicycle for your trip is the one that suits your specific needs and pocketbook. There are a great variety of bicycles available at a wide range of prices, so do some comparison shopping and some test riding.

Mountain bikes are great for the ascents and descents of mountainous terrain, and their wider tires provide greater safety; however, the thin-tired bicycles are faster on the flat. Upright handlebars provide better control and are easier on the back, but they increase the wind resistance. If speed is important, then dropped handlebars will appeal to you; triathlon-style aero handlebars are best for speed. Mountain bikes are best for backcountry cycling. Remember that a lighter bicycle with several gears will provide you with greater flexibility for climbing mountains and speeding along on long stretches of flat road.

Check out reputable bike stores that guarantee their bicycles and provide service by trained personnel on their premises. The staff will help you find the best bicycle for your needs.

If your budget is very limited, bike shops sometimes carry good used bicycles that they have overhauled. It is also possible to rent bicycles and accessories in many areas.

Bike Gear

Panniers (saddlebags) attach to carriers (racks) and hang alongside the wheel. The better panniers are waterproof;

some come with safety reflectors. Front and rear panniers are available; they must be secured so that they don't interfere with the operation of the bike. Front and rear carriers are also available; front carriers attach to the front forks; good rear carriers attach to both seat stays and have two or more supports on each side to handle the weight of the panniers.

Pack panniers so that the heaviest items are at the bottom; this will provide a lower center of gravity and a safer ride. Handlebar bags are designed for lighter items that you wish to reach quickly; the top of the handlebar bag usually contains a clear plastic map case so that you can refer to your map while riding.

A bike horn or bell is required in Canada. A battery-operated light (which can also be used as a flashlight) is also a useful purchase and is necessary if cycling at night or through dark tunnels.

A theft can ruin your trip, so it is important to purchase a good bike lock. Secure your bicycle whenever you leave it, and carry valuables with you. If staying in a motel, insist on taking the bicycle into the room with you. Other precautions include scratching your name and phone number on the bike's frame, recording the bike's serial number, taking a photo of the bike (for identifying it), and adding your bike to your household insurance.

A good bicycle seat will add to your comfort and, thus, your enjoyment of the trip. Many quality seats are now on the market. The seat (saddle) is at the proper height when you can sit on it with one foot touching the ground. A properly adjusted seat is essential for your speed and comfort (neck and back injuries can result from a badly adjusted seat).

Proper cycling apparel is essential. A good pair of shoes, gloves, and pants (properly fitting, and padded, so that you avoid blistering), sunglasses, and a properly fitting helmet will all add to your comfort. Using a glo-vest will make you more visible while riding in traffic and at night. Refer to the list on page 23 for the tools and spares you should carry, especially on a long tour.

If breakdowns occur, don't panic. Be prepared for minor problems (such as flat tires and slipping chains). To avoid greasy hands, you can use old socks on your hands, or pack rubber gloves. After a breakdown or problem, check things out at a bike shop at your earliest convenience.

Planning Your Trip

Careful planning is essential, especially for longer trips. Find out as much as you can about your planned route (the road conditions, width of paved shoulder, accommodations available, etc.). This book is intended to help you with this planning. You might also contact the tourism centers in the designated area. If you are a member of an automobile club (such as the Canadian Automobile Association or the American Automobile Association), the club can provide you with maps and information.

You can purchase bicycle touring maps through such bicycle organizations as the Canadian Cycling Association and Adventure Cycling in the U.S. Addresses and phone numbers are included for each province in Chapters 4–14, which describe specific recommended tours; hotline numbers for each province and the Territories are found in the Appendix.

Plan your routes pouring over maps and other information, studying routes; however, maintain a flexibility so that you can change your route, even during your trip, after talking to locals. It is a good idea to have an inclination as to your destination for each day so that you can arrange for motels, camping facilities, etc.

By carrying the proper equipment (including repair kit, clothes, and supplies) and carefully planning your trip, there is less stress on you during your ride.

Another part of good planning for a longer trip is proper conditioning. Don't just decide to set out on a long journey without doing some training and preparation for the ride. Build up some miles on your bicycle by going on regular, short journeys; include some longer routes, too. Get your body accustomed to the cycling. Proper exercise and diet will also help to prepare your body. Most important of all, psychologically prepare yourself (if you are determined to complete a particular ride, then you probably will).

What To Pack For Your Bicycle Trip

Your touring plans will dictate what gear is essential. If you plan to camp out and cook, then a stove, tent, and sleeping bag are essential items; however, if you plan to stop at motels or bed-and-breakfast inns, and eat in restaurants, the required load becomes much lighter.

Clothing may vary depending on your planned route, but a general rule is to carry as little as possible. Take wash-and-wear clothing. Even in summer, it is best to wear layers of clothing. Begin with proper underwear that prevents moisture from being trapped against your skin; you can then wear another shirt, sweater, and a nylon windbreaker in succeeding layers; as you warm up, simply remove the outer layer.

Finally, here is a list of the items you may want to carry, depending on the conditions of your specific trip.

Bicycle Gear:

bicycle helmet
carriers and panniers
handlebar bag with map pouch
battery-operated light
horn or bell
tire pump
lock

rearview mirror
tire pump
cycling gloves
reflective safety vest
water bottle(s)
odometer
tool kit and spare parts

Tool Kit:

freewheel remover
tire patch kit
spoke tightener
chain lubricant
chain tool
spare inner tube
rag/clothpliers

knife
nylon cord
bungee cords
tape
screwdrivers
tire levers
wrenches and Allen keys

Additional Bike Gear:

(if room is available)
pressure gauge
extra spokes
spare brake shoes
spare brake and gear cables

spare chain links
spare nuts and bolts
spare batteries and bulb for
    your light

Clothing:

shorts
bike shorts
long-sleeved shirt
shirts
sweater
nylon windbreaker
rain gear

swimming trunks/suit
thermal tights and shirt
socks
underwear
sweat pants
slacks/long pants/skirts

Supplies:

toothbrush and toothpaste
soap and towel
pocket knife
sunglasses
sunscreen
insect repellent
razor
comb/brush
watch

credit cards
money
liniment
camera and film
notebook and pen
maps
first aid kit (including lip
    balm, bandages, antiseptic,
    pain relief)

Camping Supplies:

(if you will be camping out)
tent
ground sheet
sleeping bag
pots
food containers
food
dishes

cutlery
fuel
stove
matches
can opener
dish cloth, towel
scouring pad
dishwashing liquid

CHAPTER 4

Alberta

Alberta has a great variety of terrain suitable for exploration by bicycle. The tours described in this book focus on the magnificence of Alberta's mountains. Many of the roads have a wide paved shoulder. Since you will be cycling in mountainous terrain, the summer is the best time of year for this trip. Although it is possible to encounter a sudden snowstorm at any time, the average temperature range in the summer is 5°C to 24°C (40°F to 75°F).

Several Alberta cities have an urban trail system that is designed with cyclists in mind. Both Edmonton and Calgary have such a system. Alberta Transportation and Utilities provides a map for cyclists; it includes information on the condition of the road pavement and the width of the road shoulder. Contact:

Alberta Travel and Utilities
Twin Atria Bldg.
9999 - 98th Ave.
Edmonton, Alberta T6B 2X3
Telephone (403) 427-7674

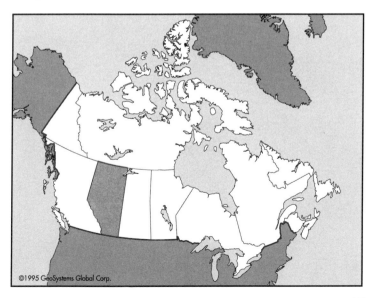

©1995 GeoSystems Global Corp.

For more information:

Alberta Bed and Breakfast
4327 - 86th St.
Edmonton, Alberta 6K 1A9
Telephone (403) 462-8885

The Alberta Bicycle Vacation
Guide
960 2 - 80th Ave.
Edmonton, Alberta T6C 0V3

Alberta Bicycling Association
11759 Groat Road
Edmonton, Alberta T5M 3K6
Telephone (403) 453-8518
FAX (403) 453-8553

Alberta Tourism
10155 - 102nd St.
Edmonton, Alberta T5J 4L6
Telephone (403) 427-4321 or
1-800-661-1222

Bed and Breakfast Bureau
Station E
Calgary, Alberta T3C 3L8;
Telephone (403) 242-5555

Hostelling International
No. 203
1414 Kensington Road N.W,
Calgary, Alberta T2N 3P9
Telephone (403) 283-5551

The Icefields Parkway

Distance: 290 km (180 mi.)

Duration: 3–5 days

Rating: strenuous

Type: one-way tour

Access:

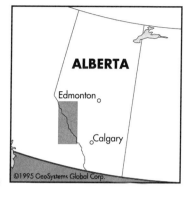

Both Jasper and Banff have Via Rail Service. Bus service is offered from the Calgary airport to Banff and Jasper; phone 1-800-332-1419.

Accommodations

The Alberta Hostelling Association operates a number of hostels along the Icefields Parkway. Reservations are advised in the summer.

There are several campgrounds and hostels along the route. Whistlers and Wapiti campgrounds and Whistlers Mountain Hostel are located near Jasper; phone (403) 439-3089 for hostel reservations.

Banff has a campground and hostel on Tunnel Mountain Road; phone (403) 762-4122 for hostel reservations. Full services are available at Banff and Jasper.

Route Description:

Arguably the greatest cycling tour in North America, the Icefields Parkway connects Jasper and Banff. You cycle on a wide paved shoulder amid beautiful scenery and an abundance of wildlife. You will find several hostels and campgrounds as you ride from Jasper to Banff; however, there are few grocery stores or restaurants and lots of traffic.

Jasper Provincial Park is home to many species of wildlife, including overly bold bears. They frequent garbage dumps; be cautious with your food. Depart from Jasper on No. 93, passing the two campgrounds at Whistlers and Wapiti. The road is rather gentle, at first, as you follow the Athabasca River and pass Athabasca Falls. You ascend to Athabasca Glacier and Sunwapta Pass.

The Columbia Icefield, the largest icecap south of the Arctic, is accessible. You can walk up to the icefield or take a ride by snowcoach out onto it. Visit the Information Center to learn more about this phenomenon. The glorious peaks of Mount Athabasca and Mount Kitchener tower over this area. It is about 110 km (65 mi.) from Jasper to the Columbia Icefields and about 180 km (110 mi.) from the Columbia Icefields to Banff.

From the glacier, the route passes two more campgrounds and tackles the last slopes of Sunwapta Pass. Near the summit, you enter Banff National Park, the oldest park in

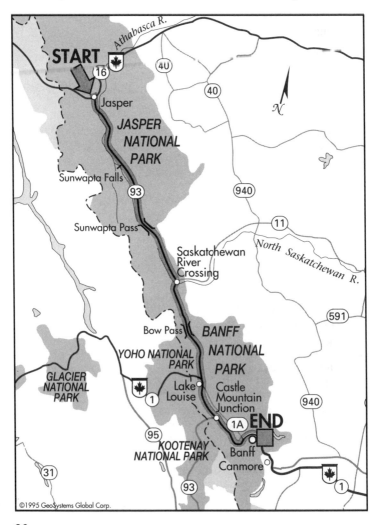

Canada. If the weather is good, take a hike on Parker Ridge, above the tree line; the bare ridge overlooks the peaks of the icefield area and provides an excellent view of the Saskatchewan Glacier, which is even larger than the Athabasca Glacier.

Dress warmly for the long descent into the valley of the North Saskatchewan River (where a nice hiking trail leads to Bridal Veil Falls). There is a long curve at the bottom of the hill, and the grade becomes gentler as you follow the North Saskatchewan River through Graveyard Flats to Rampart Creek. The route gradually descends past the high limestone cliffs of Mount Wilson, past the turnoff for the David Thompson Highway, to the North Saskatchewan River crossing.

The road climbs as you follow the Mistaya River. You will pass Waterfowl Lake and Snowbird Glacier Viewpoint, and then the road becomes especially steep (for about the last 7 km/4 mi.) until you reach the Bow Summit. For a spectacular view, hike to Peyto Glacier (about a 10-minute walk); below, you will see the beautiful opaque blue-green of glacier-fed Peyto Lake and the long Mistaya Valley (which you have just ascended).

Bow Summit divides the North and South Saskatchewan river systems. From your location at the Bow Summit, there is a glorious downhill ride. Take time to admire Bow Lake and Hector Lake as you descend to Lake Louise. You can hike on one of the best glacier trails in the Rockies: Plain of the Six Glaciers. You can even stop at a teahouse at the end of this 5.5 km (3.5 mi.) trail.

Since you are now in the heart of the Rocky Mountains tourist area, be prepared to pay more for accommodations (in the Lake Louise–Banff area) and to face more traffic.

Complete this picturesque tour by cycling from Lake Louise to Banff (described in Chapter 15).

Side trip to Red Deer:

Exit the Icefields Parkway at Saskatchewan River Crossing, and take the David Thompson Highway (No. 11) to Red Deer, where you can visit Waskasoo Park, with its more than 45 km/27 mi. of bicycle, pedestrian, and equestrian trails. This route has limited services.

Backcountry Cycling:

For trails and fire roads available for backcountry cycling in
Banff, Kootenay, Waterton Lakes, Yoho, Jasper, and
Revelstoke National Parks, contact:

Trail Bicycling in National Parks in Alberta and B.C.
Canadian Parks Service
Western Regional Office
P.O. Box 2989, Station M
Calgary, Alberta T2P 3H8
Telephone (403) 292-4401

Ride from Jasper to Mount Robson:

This 83 km (50 mi.) ride takes you to the Yellowhead Pass,
one of the lowest passes on the Continental Divide (and,
therefore, not a strenuous climb) and to the Mount Robson
viewpoint. Mount Robson is the highest peak in the
Canadian Rockies.

Ride from Jasper to Edmonton:

This hilly route (345 km/207 mi.) will take you on the
Yellowhead Highway (with a wide paved shoulder) to
Alberta's capital. Edmonton has a wonderful network of
bicycle routes and paths. For a *Cycle Edmonton Map and
Information Guide*, contact:

Edmonton Transportation Department
10th Floor, Century Place
9803 - 102A Ave.
Edmonton, Alberta T5J 3R5
Telephone (403) 428-4735

Optional Activities:

Hiking trails include:
> trail to Buck and Osprey Lakes
> trails near the Icefield (including Wilcox Pass and Hilda
> Creek)
> Parker Ridge Trail (above the tree line—5 km/3 mi. round
> trip)
> trail to Bridal Veil Falls Mistaya Canyon trail
> trails near Waterfowl Lake
> trail to Peyto Glacier (at the Bow Summit)
> Glacier trail at Lake Louise (with a teahouse at the end of

the 5.5 km/3.5 mi. trail) provides a view of six glaciers
trails in Johnston Canyon

For more information:

Banff National Park Information, including the Trail
Bicycling Guide; phone (403) 762-4256.

Superintendent	Superintendent
Banff National Park	Jasper National Park
P.O. Box 900	P.O. Box 10
Banff, Alberta T0L 0C0	Jasper, Alberta T0E 1E0
Telephone (403) 762-4256	Telephone (604) 566-4325

The Golden Triangle

Distance: 313 km (195 mi.)

Duration: 3–5 days

Rating: strenuous

Type: loop route

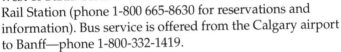

Access:

Castle Mountain Junction is located just 31 km (18 mi.) west of Banff. Banff has a Via Rail Station (phone 1-800 665-8630 for reservations and information). Bus service is offered from the Calgary airport to Banff—phone 1-800-332-1419.

Accommodations:

Castle Mountain Hostel; phone for reservations through the Calgary office at (403) 283-5551.

Castle Mountain Village chalets; phone (403) 762-3311.

There are several campgrounds along the route. Full services are available at Radium Hot Springs, Golden, and Lake Louise.

A campground and a hostel are located on Tunnel Mountain Road; phone (403) 762-4122 for hostel reservations.

Route Description

For a magnificent view of the Canadian Rockies, try this extended tour through three mountain passes and three spectacular national parks. Bisect the Continental Divide twice as you ride in two provinces through the scenic marvels of this peak-rimmed loop tour. You will cycle from Castle Mountain Junction to Radium Hot Springs, to Golden, and back to Castle Mountain Junction.

The Golden Triangle is Alberta's largest organized yearly trip; Calgary's Elbow Valley Cycle Club organizes this event, which attracts a large number of cyclists each spring. Of course, you can enjoy this adventure at any time.

Begin this loop tour at Castle Mountain Junction, 30 km (18 mi.) west of Banff, Alberta. Take the overpass above the

Trans Canada Highway to No. 93, and then begin the long climb to the Vermilion Pass. There is a wide paved shoulder as you cycle on this mountain highway and cross the Continental Divide. At the Continental Divide, you can take the Fireweed Trail to view the effects of a 1968 forest fire. Storm Mountain Lodge is located at the top of the pass. At the Vermilion Pass, waters to the west run to the Pacific Ocean by way of the Columbia River; waters to the east flow into the Bow River and, ultimately, Hudson Bay.

You cycle in Kootenay National Park as you ride through Marble Canyon, Vermilion River, Hector Gorge, where there is a steep uphill to a viewpoint; and McLeod Meadows, where a campground is located. You then face another steep climb to a view of the Kootenay Valley from the summit of Sinclair Pass. Watch for mountain goats, bighorn sheep, deer, moose, bear, and elk.

From the Sinclair Pass, descend through a long, narrow canyon, past the Iron Gates (limestone and dolomite cliffs colored by hot mineral waters) to Radium Hot Springs, where you can relax in hot springs at the Aquacourt.

Turn north on No. 95, and ride through farmland and small hamlets through the Columbia River Valley to Golden. Strong headwinds can pose a problem; take care in this section, as the paved shoulder disappears in places.

Join the Trans Canada Highway (No. 1) at Golden, and head east. There are some long, steep climbs, before you enter Yoho National Park. (*Yoho* is the Cree word for awe, which is very appropriate for this magnificent area.) Continue cycling to Field. Here you have the toughest of the climbs as you cycle through the Kicking Horse Pass, straddling the Continental Divide. Be prepared for a series of strenuous, challenging switchbacks as you climb toward the summit. Stop to view the Spiral Train Tunnels near the summit, which will add to your appreciation of the engineering involved in crossing the Kicking Horse Pass by train.

Cross the border from the province of British Columbia into Alberta, and descend on No. 1. Veer off on No. 1A to beautiful Lake Louise, with its background of white-peaked mountains. You then face a sharp descent, on switchbacks, as you ride from the lake to the townsite.

Continue on No. 1A (the Bow Valley Parkway) in Banff National Park to the end of the loop tour at Castle Mountain Junction. There is no paved shoulder on No. 1A, but the traffic will be lighter than on the Trans Canada Highway.

Side trip to Takakkaw Falls:

You will find the turnoff for Takakkaw Falls just past Field. The return trip is about 30 km (18 mi.). There is not a paved shoulder, and the road is narrow and steep; however, the road does have a good paved surface, and the falls are

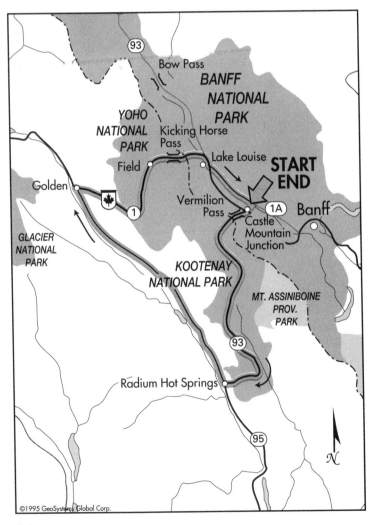

©1995 GeoSystems Global Corp.

magnificent. There is a campground and a vast network of trails here.

For trails and fire roads available for backcountry cycling in Banff, Kootenay, Waterton Lakes, Yoho, Jasper, and Revelstoke National Parks, contact:
Trail Bicycling in National Parks in Alberta and B.C.
Canadian Parks Service
Western Regional Office
PO Box 2989, Station M
Calgary, Alberta T2P 3H8
Telephone (403) 292-4401.

Ride to Cranbrook, British Columbia:

From Radium Hot Springs, cycle south on No. 95 to Invermere, Fairmont Hot Springs, Canal Flats, and Skookumchuk. Take No. 95A to Kimberley (with its Bavarian-style downtown), and continue this journey to Cranbrook, in the eastern Kootenays. This route has a wide paved shoulder and is popular with tourists; there are spectacular views. Flights are available from Cranbrook.

Cycling into Drumheller, in the Alberta badlands.

Optional Activities:

Hiking trails include:
> the Fireweed Trail (to view the effects of a forest fire)
> Vista Lake Viewpoint (about a 90-minute walk near the summit of Vermilion Pass to Vista Lake and back)
> a short, interpretive nature trail at the summit of Vermilion Pass
> interpretive trail at Paint Pots (1.6 km/1 mi.)

Canoeing on the Bow River, near Banff, is a unique way to truly appreciate the gentle, glacier-carved Bow Valley.

For more information:

Banff National Park Information, including the Trail Bicycling Guide, phone (403) 762-4256.

Elbow Valley Cycle Club
225 10th St. NW
Calgary, Alberta T2V 1V5

Superintendent
Banff National Park
Box 900
Banff, Alberta T0L 0C0
Telephone (403) 762-3324

Superintendent
Kootenay National Park
Box 220
Radium Hot Springs, B.C.
V0A 1M0
Telephone (604) 347-9615

Waterton Lakes National Park

Distance: 31 km (19 mi.)

Duration: 1 day

Rating: strenuous

Type: return trip

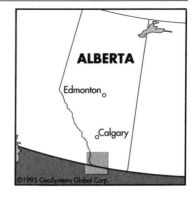

Access:

During the summer, buses serve the park from Pincher Creek, Alberta, and from Great Falls and Kalispell, Montana.

Accommodations:

There are several hotels in the village of Waterton. Full services are available. There is camping in Waterton Lakes National Park.

Bike Rental

Mountain bikes can be rented from Pat's Texaco in Waterton; phone (403) 859-2266 for reservations.

Route Description:

Situated in Alberta's southwest corner (near Montana's border and adjoining Glacier National Park) is beautiful Waterton Lakes National Park (264 km/158 mi. southwest of Calgary). Since there is no main highway through the park, traffic tends to be much lighter than in the better-known parks, Jasper and Banff. There is an excellent opportunity for seeing wildlife in Waterton Lakes National Park, and the wildflower display is magnificent. However, all the short trips from Waterton begin with a steep climb, the road has no paved shoulder, and the headwinds can be very irritating.

One recommended trip in Waterton Lakes National Park takes you from Waterton to Cameron Lake and back. The Akamina Parkway leads through the historic Cameron Valley to spectacular views, and the valley helps to protect your from the sometimes brutal headwinds.

The toughest part of this trip is the climb out of Waterton. Then the road levels off as you follow Cameron Creek. You will see a plaque that commemorates the spot where oil was discovered in 1901. The road gradually climbs to the Akamina Pass and Cameron Lake.

There are several interesting hiking trails in the park, and there are canoe rentals and an interpretive center at Cameron Lake. The international boundary between the United States and Canada bisects this lake near the base of Mount Custer. The Cameron Lake region is home to birds rarely seen in other areas of Waterton Lakes National Park, such as Steller's jay and the varied thrush. Immense 500-year-old spruce trees can be observed here, too. The area's meadows are prime grizzly bear habitat.

The return trip to Waterton includes some nice descents.

Ride to Lethbridge:

From Waterton, cycle north on No. 6 and east on No. 3 or north on No. 6 and northeast on No. 5 to Lethbridge, a meatpacking and grain distribution center. You might like to

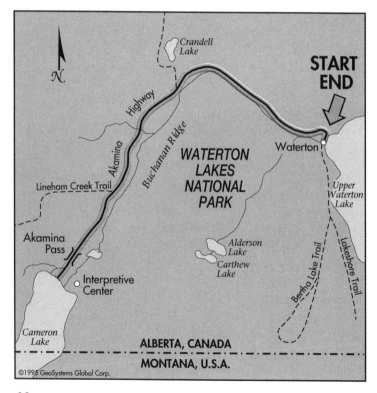

visit such points of interest as Indian Battle Park, site of the last intertribal battle in North America—between the Blackfoot and the Cree; Brewery Gardens, with special floral displays; Nikka Yuko Japanese Gardens, one of the most authentic of its type in North America; and the Sir Alexander Galt Museum and Archives, with a history of the Lethbridge area.

Ride through the Crowsnest Pass:

From Lethbridge, cycle north on No. 6 and west on No. 3; you will have a tough climb as you ascend the Crowsnest Pass. You then cross the border and descend into British Columbia (it's about 1,100 km/660 mi. from Waterton, Alberta, to Vancouver, B.C.).

Cycle into Glacier National Park:

Cross the border from Canada into the United States, from Alberta into Montana, and cycle south on No. 17 and No. 89 to St. Mary. Then ride west into the park, with its spectacular views on the Going-To-The-Sun Highway. Waterton Lakes and Glacier National Parks are known together as the Waterton-Glacier International Peace Park.

Optional Activities:

Hiking trails include:
  Bears Hump Trail Lakeshore Trail 2 km (1.2 mi.)
  Hike to Crandell Lake
  Lineham Creek Trail
  Rowe Lakes Trail

For information on trails and fire roads available for backcountry cycling in Banff, Kootenay, Waterton Lakes, Yoho, Jasper, and Revelstoke National Parks, contact:

Trail Bicycling in National Parks in Alberta and B.C.
Canadian Parks Service
Western Regional Office
P.O. Box 2989, Station M
Calgary, Alberta T2P 3H8
Telephone (403) 292-4401

For more information:

Chinook Country Tourist
Association
2805 Scenic Drive
Lethbridge, Alberta T0K 2M0
Telephone 1-800-661-1222

Waterton Lakes National Park
Waterton Park, Alberta T0K
2M0
Telephone (403) 859-2224

Kananaskis Country

Distance: 210 km (130 mi.)

Duration: 3–6 days

Rating: strenuous

Type: loop route

Access:

Seebe is located at the junction of the Trans Canada Highway (No. 1) and No. 40, 23 km (14 mi.) east of Canmore and 61 km (38 mi.) west of Calgary. Flights are available to Calgary. Buses are available to Seebe and Canmore.

Accommodations:

Full services are available at both Calgary and Canmore. Campgrounds are available in the parks.

Bike Rental:

Mountain bikes can be rented at Boulton Trading Post and the Mount Kidd Campground.

Route Description:

Kananaskis Country was designed for the enjoyment of cyclists, and it consists of five areas: Peter Lougheed Provincial Park; Bow Valley Provincial Park; East Kananaskis Country; Spring Lakes/Ribbon Creek areas; and Cataract Creek/Highwood areas.

The Kananaskis Trail (No. 40), the highest paved road in Canada, provides a spectacular trip through a magnificent mountain recreation area along the eastern seaboard of Banff National Park (just 100 km/60 mi. west of Calgary). This scenic route takes you through the Kananaskis Valley, cycling on an excellent, wide paved shoulder.

Begin your journey at Seebe, at the junction of the Trans Canada Highway (No. 1) and No. 40 (61 km/38 mi. west of Calgary). Head south on No. 40 past Barrier Lake, Kananaskis Forest Experimental Station (with its self-guided trails), O'Shaugnessy Falls, the Kananaskis Golf Course,

Mount Kidd Recreational Vehicle Park (open to tenters), and the Fortress Mountain ski area, to Peter Lougheed Provincial Park.

Campgrounds, paved bicycle trails, and mountain bike trails are all available in Peter Lougheed Provincial Park. The Visitor Centers have information and bike trail maps. Paved bike trails include the 5 km (3 mi.) Evan Thomas Trail and the 5 km (3 mi.) Lodgepole Trail. Backcountry routes in Kananaskis Country include the 10 km (6 mi.) Carnarvon Lake Trail and the 19 km (12 mi.) Skogan Pass Trail from Dead Man's Flat to Ribbon Creek. A popular 2-day

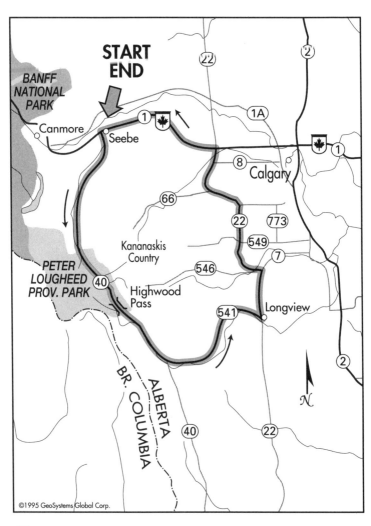

©1995 GeoSystems Global Corp.

backcountry circuit includes parts of the Big Elbow Trail, Sheep River Trail, and Forget-Me-Not Ridge.

After exploring the trails of Peter Lougheed Provincial Park, continue south on No. 40 as it ascends through the meadows and mountain scenery to the summit of Highwood Pass (Canada's highest paved road). At the summit is Highwood Meadows, with two interpretive trails.

Continuing on No. 40, descend along the Highwood River and gradually emerge from the mountains to the foothills as you arrive in ranching country. Turn east onto No. 541 at Highwood Junction, 37 km (23 mi.) from Highwood Pass. Leaving Kananaskis Country, cycle on No. 541 to Longview (43 km/26 mi. from Highwood Junction). Turn north on No. 22 (which has narrow shoulders) to Black Diamond, Turner Valley, Millarville, and Bragg Creek. Return to the Trans Canada Highway (No. 1), and cycle west to Seebe to complete this loop tour.

Ride to Calgary:

At Bragg Creek, leave the described loop tour and cycle northeast on No. 22 and east on No. 8 into Calgary. Calgary has a well-signed 90 km (54 mi.) on-street bikeway system, which takes the cyclist on low- traffic and residential roads. Calgary also offers a corridor of paved trails and bicycle commuter routes.

For a copy of *Cycle Route Map: A Guide to Calgary's Pathways and Bikeways*, contact:

The City of Calgary
Telephone (403) 268-1574 or (403) 221-3999.

Ride to Drumheller:

Visit the fascinating Alberta Badlands by cycling east from Calgary on No. 1 to No. 9; then ride northeast on No. 9 to Drumheller 138 km (77 mi.), known as Dinosaur Country. This trip has been previously described in Part II.

Optional Activities:

There are several bike trails at the Canmore Nordic Centre (including two novice mountain bike loops and a trail to the Banff Park boundary). Trail maps are available from:

The Canmore Nordic Centre
Box 1979
Canmore, Alberta T0L 0M0
Telephone (403) 678-2400

Hiking trails in Kananaskis Country include:
   Valleyview Trail (steep grade, from the Visitor Center in
      Peter Lougheed Provincial Park—9km/6 mi.)
   Rock Glacier Nature Trail (near the summit of Highwood
      Pass)
   Cirque Trail (a 5 km/3 mi. hike through an ancient forest)
   Etherington Creek hiking trails
   Centennial Trail
   North Kananaskis Trail

Whitewater rafting, horseback riding, heli-hiking, helicopter
sightseeing tours, and heli-biking are all available in the area.

For more information:

Calgary Bicycle Advisory
Council
1111 Memorial Drive NW
Calgary, Alberta T2N 3E4
Telephone (403) 270-2262

Kananaskis Country
Box 280
Canmore, Alberta T0L 0M0
Telephone (403) 678-5508

Kananaskis Country
Suite 412
1011 Glenmore Trail SW
Calgary, Alberta T2V 4R6
Telephone (403) 297-3362

Peter Lougheed Prov. Park
Telephone (403) 591-7222

Chapter 5

British Columbia

As you cycle through British Columbia's mountainous terrain, you will be pleased to find wide paved shoulders. You will also meet many other cyclists, as this is a very popular activity amid the spectacular mountain scenery.

Canada's westernmost province tends to receive its fair share of rain, particularly on the coast, so don't forget your rain gear. For cycling through the mountain passes, it's best to dress in layers to cope with drastic temperature variations.

In this chapter, 3 different rides are described, ranging from a little over 100 km to more than 400 km in length.

For more information:

Bicycling Association of BC
No. 332 - 1367 W. Broadway
Vancouver, B.C. V6H 4A9
Telephone (604) 737-3034
FAX (604) 738-7175
Ride hotline: (604) 290-0455

Vancouver Travel Infocentre
812 Wharf St.
Victoria, B.C. V7X 1L3
Telephone (604) 683-2000

©1995 GeoSystems Global Corp.

Tunnel entrance in Fraser Canyon, British Columbia. Take off your sunglasses, turn on your lights, and ride carefully.

Hostelling International
B.C. Region
No. 402 - 134 Abbott St.
Vancouver, B.C. V6B 2K4
Telephone (604) 684-7101
FAX (604) 684-7181

Ministry of Tourism
Parliament Building
Victoria, B.C. V8V 1X4
Telephone (604) 382-2127

British Columbia's Gulf Islands

Distance   251 km (157 mi.)

Duration: 5–7 days

Rating: moderate

Type: loop route

Access:

Tsawwasen is located 29 km (18 mi.) west of Vancouver. A shuttle service is available through the George Massey Tunnel, as cycling is not allowed; phone (604) 277-2115 to confirm the schedule. For 24-hour information on the mainland–Vancouver Island ferries, phone (604) 669-1211 (Vancouver); (604) 277-2115 (Victoria). There are international airports at both Vancouver and Victoria.

Accommodations:

Full services are available in Vancouver and Victoria. There are several campgrounds, including: McDonald Park, near the Swartz Bay Ferry Terminal; Montague Harbour Marine Park, on Galiano Island; and Ruckle Park and Mowat Park, both on Saltspring Island.

Route Description:

One of the west coast's most spectacular cycling areas, the Gulf Islands comprise approximately one hundred enchanting islands on the west coast of the Strait of Georgia. Many of these islands are linked by ferry. Island roads tend to be quite narrow and hilly, but traffic is usually light.

From Tsawwasen, B.C., you can take a ferry to Swartz Bay on Vancouver Island. Cycle on No. 17 to Victoria. There are few hills on this route, and the road condition and shoulders are very good. Traffic may be heavy, but you will feel right at home because of the great number of cyclists here.

While in Victoria, enjoy its scenic seaport location and quaint British charm. You may choose to visit the Provincial Parliament Buildings, Royal British Columbia Museum,

Maritime Museum of British Columbia, and the Butchart Gardens.

Returning to Swartz Bay, take the ferry to Fulford Harbour on Saltspring Island. The island is 75 km (45 mi.) long, and you can explore this picturesque island by bicycle; you will find some steep climbs.

Other Gulf Islands accessible by ferry include Saturna (35 km/21 mi. long), Pender (43 km/26 mi.), Galiano (75 km/45 mi.), and Mayne (33 km/20 mi.). Mayne Island was the first place apples were grown in British Columbia;

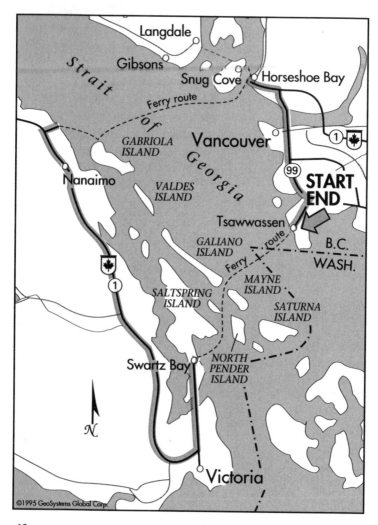

many miners stopped at Miner's Bay on this island during the Gold Rush.

Return to the mainland to complete this loop tour.

Alternate route to Victoria:

There will be less traffic noise if you cycle from Swartz Bay through Sidney, on No. 17A.

Ride to Nanaimo:

Cycle north on No. 1 from Victoria to Nanaimo and Departure Bay about 115 km (69 mi.). You can then take a ferry back to the mainland, arriving at Horseshoe Bay (near Vancouver).

Explore Gabriola Island:

A 20-minute ferry ride from Nanaimo will take you to Gabriola Island, where you can cycle on a loop tour of the island (35 km/21 mi.); there are private campgrounds and lodges on this picturesque island.

Ride on the Sunshine Coast:

From Horseshoe Bay, you can take a ferry to Langdale, on the Sunshine Coast (where, ironically, it often rains). A hilly ride along the coast takes you to Gibsons, the friendly community featured in the television show *The Beachcombers*.

Ride to Pacific Rim National Park:

Cycle north on No. 19 from Nanaimo to Parksville. Then ride on the narrow, winding, hilly No. 4 west to Port Alberni and Long Beach; there are some tough climbs and switchbacks between Port Alberni and Long Beach, and there are no stores (so travel prepared). There are many good campsites at Long Beach. Cycle along the beach for 8 km (5 mi.) to the fishing village of Ucluelet, where accommodations are available. You can take a whale-watching trip from here. At Ucluelet, you can also get a ferry back to Port Alberni. This trip to the park and back to Nanaimo is about 260 km (156 mi.) of cycling, plus the ferry ride on the Alberni Inlet.

For information about the ferry, contact:

Alberni Marine Transportation Ltd.
PO Box 188
Port Alberni, BC V9Y 7M7
Telephone (604) 723-8313 or 1-800-663-7192.

For information on spectacular Pacific Rim National Park, contact:

Pacific Rim National Park
PO Box 280
Ucluelet, BC V0R 3A0
Telephone (604) 726-7721.

Ride on the Sea to Sky Highway:

If you want a very challenging series of climbs, try cycling from Vancouver to Whistler on the Sea to Sky Highway (No. 99), a one-way trip of about 110 km (66 mi.); the road climbs more than 2,000 m (6,000 ft) from sea level at Squamish to Whistler. The road has a narrow paved shoulder and is very twisty. Traffic can be heavy on this route; watch for fallen rock on the road.

For more information:

British Columbia Ferry Co.
1112 Fort St.
Victoria, BC V8V 4V2
Telephone (604) 386-3431

Victoria Travel InfoCentre
812 Wharf St.
Victoria, B.C. V8W 1T3
Telephone (604) 382-2127

Saltspring Island Chamber of Commerce Travel InfoCentre
Box 111
Ganges, BC V0S 1E0
Telephone (604) 537-5252
FAX (604) 537-4276
(Gulf Islands maps and info)

Fraser Canyon Loop Tour

Distance: 405 km (243 mi.)

Duration: 4–6 days

Rating: strenuous

Type: loop route

Access:

Hope is located 150 km (90 mi.) east of Vancouver. Buses are available. Since the Trans Canada Highway (No. 1) is off-limits to bicycles between Vancouver and Chilliwack, take No. 7 from Vancouver, following the Fraser River (the route of the explorer Simon Fraser) to Hope.

Accommodations:

Services are available at Hope, Merritt, and Princeton. Several campgrounds are available on this route, including Manning Park. Also in Manning Park is Manning Park Lodge.

Route Description:

This magnificent tour will take you from Hope, through the Fraser Canyon, to Merritt and Princeton, and back through spectacular Manning Park to Hope.

This challenging trip provides you with many memorable views of southern British Columbia. The summer alpine meadows of Manning Park contain blue lupine, yellow arnica, and red paintbrush, among others.

Take the Trans Canada Highway (No. 1) from Hope, and enter the Fraser Canyon. You have many spectacular views as you cycle through the canyon on a wide paved shoulder. There are many challenging climbs, and you cycle through several tunnels cut through the rock. Take care in these rather dangerous tunnels. They are dark, and the shoulder disappears. Remove your sunglasses, put on your bike light, wait until no traffic is coming, and then ride through the tunnels with speed.

Near Boston Bar, you can visit Hell's Gate by taking a tram down into this fantastic gorge. At Lytton, the rafting capital

51

of Canada, where the Fraser and Thomson Rivers meet, you can take a whitewater rafting excursion.

Continue north on No. 1 from Lytton to Spences Bridge, following a section of the Gold Rush Trail. At Spences Bridge, take No. 8 southeast to Merritt, through the Nicola Valley. The history of this region is chronicled in the Nicola Valley Museum Archives in Merritt.

Head southeast on No. 5A from Merritt to Princeton, passing Aspen Grove, Allison Lake Park, and Otter Lake Park. You face a very tough climb out of Merritt, and the terrain is quite hilly until you descend into Princeton.

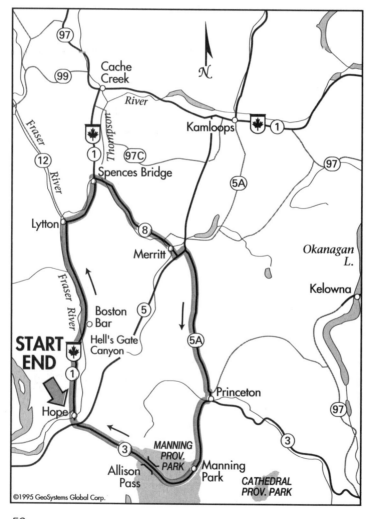

©1995 GeoSystems Global Corp.

Take No. 3 southwest from Princeton. There are a couple of very difficult climbs as you cycle through Manning Park (Sunday Summit and Allison Pass). This is the toughest part of this trip, and you will find very few facilities along this section of the Princeton-Hope Highway, so travel prepared. Some cyclists maintain that the section through Manning Park is as challenging as any section found in the entire country. After reaching the summit of Allison Pass, you can luxuriate in the splendor of a long descent. Once you are through Manning Park, you follow the Skagit River and travel through the Skagit Valley Recreation Area as you cycle toward Hope, the destination of this loop tour.

Alternate cycling route:

Take the Coquihalla Highway (No. 5) from Hope to Merritt. This route avoids cycling through the picturesque but rather dangerous Fraser Canyon. This alternate route to Merritt has a wide paved shoulder but more traffic.

Optional Activities:

At Hell's Gate, take a tram down into the fantastic gorge.

Whitewater rafting excursions are available in the Lytton area.

In Merritt, visit the Nicola Valley Museum Archives to learn the history of this region.

There are extensive hiking trails in Manning Park. You might like to take a side trip to Lightning Lake or Gibson's Pass (ski area). A footpath leads through mauve-colored flowers at Rhododendron Flats. Horse rentals and nature programs are also available in the park.

Kootenay Lake

Distance   115 km (69 mi.)

Duration: 1–2 days

Rating: moderate

Type: one-way tour

Access:

Buses are available in Nelson
and Creston. There is air
service in nearby Cranbrook.

BRITISH
COLUMBIA

Victoria   Vancouver

©1995 GeoSystems Global Corp.

Accommodations:

Nelson has a City Tourist Park, overlooking a lake. For
reservations, phone (604) 354-4944. Full services are available
in Nelson and Creston. There are several campgrounds and
resorts along this route.

Route Description:

This scenic tour of peaks, forests, and orchards, as you
journey around a large section of Kootenay Lake, is
tailor-made for cycling. There are some climbs, but most of
the trip is relatively easy, with rolling hills. The roads are
rather narrow, but they are in good condition, and traffic is
relatively light. Headwinds may be a problem.

Begin your tour in Nelson, the Queen City of the Kootenays.
Nelson had its beginnings in 1887 when silver was
discovered on Toad Mountain. Nelson has over 350 heritage
buildings, many restored to their original splendor from the
days of the silver boom (the town's architecture was featured
in *Roxanne*, a film starring Daryl Hannah and Steve Martin).

Cycle northeast on No. 3A for 35 km (21 mi.). Ride through
Willow Point and Kokanee Creek Provincial Park (which has
camping and several beaches) to Balfour, departure point for
the longest free ferry ride in North America (a very
picturesque trip, with snow-capped mountains in the
distance).

After the 40-minute ferry crossing from Balfour to Kootenay
Bay, there is a tough climb to Crawford Bay. Then the riding
is hilly, but the grade remains quite easy as you follow the

eastern shore of Kootenay Lake. You pass many beaches, campgrounds, and scenic spots as you cycle to Gray Creek, Boswell, and Destiny Bay. Stop at the Glass House (made of embalming fluid bottles) south of Boswell. As you continue cycling through Sanca, Sirdar, and Wynndel (with climbs out of Sirdar and Wynndel), you eventually leave the lake and enter the wide, flat Creston Valley.

Cycling is very easy as you pass the orchards of the fertile Creston Valley. Your tour ends as you meet No. 3 and ride into Creston. There are several fruit stands as you cycle in the Creston area.

The Creston Valley Wildlife Centre is home to 250 species of birds and has the highest density of osprey in the world.

Ride to mines and ghost towns:

For a challenging loop tour that takes you through a once-famous mining area, cycle north from Balfour on No. 31. Zinc and lead were discovered near Ainsworth Hot

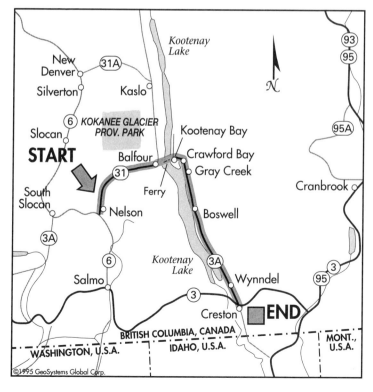

Springs. Near Kaslo, a very valuable ore boulder was discovered in 1892, and Kaslo quickly prospered. Sandon was the site of a huge silver strike; this boomtown has little left today (it was also the site of a Japanese internment camp during World War II).

Cycle south on No. 6 to New Denver. Once the center for recording mine claims in the Slocan area, Silverton offers spectacular views of abandoned silver mines from the summit above the town. Slocan, once a city of over 6,000, now claims to be the smallest incorporated city in the world. Take No. 3A back to Nelson to complete this loop tour.

Nelson–Kootenay Lake cycling loop tour:

At Creston, take No. 3 west to Salmo. Then ride north on No. 6 back to Nelson. This added 122 km (73 mi.) will make the original, detailed tour a loop tour.

Ride to Cranbrook:

Take No. 3 from Creston to Cranbrook 106 km (66 mi.). Air service is available here.

Optional Activities:

Dine on a verandah at Destiny Bay (Destiny Bay Resort).

Visit the Glass House (near Destiny Bay), where funeral director David Brown constructed a house, along the shore of Kootenay Lake, from a collection of empty embalming fluid bottles.

For more information:

Nelson Travel InfoCentre
225 Hall St.
Nelson, B.C. V1L 5X4
Telephone (604) 352-3433

Manitoba

Manitoba is dotted with a great number of crystal-clear lakes. One of them, Lake Winnipeg, is the fifth largest in Canada (larger than Lake Ontario). The varied terrain of this prairie province ranges from grain-rich plains in the south, to tundra and boreal forest in the north, to rolling, wooded areas and grasslands in the central region.. Average summer temperatures for Manitoba range from about 10°C (50°F) at night to 25°C (77°F) during the day.

For more information:

Canadian Hostelling Assoc. Manitoba Inc. 194A Sherbrooke St. Winnipeg, Manitoba R3C 2B6 Telephone (204) 784-1131

Manitoba Cycling Association 200 Main St. Winnipeg, Manitoba R3C 4M2 Telephone (204) 985-4055 FAX (204) 985-4223

Travel Manitoba 7-155 Carlton St. Winnipeg, Manitoba R3C 3H8 Telephone 1-800-665-0040

©1995 GeoSystems Global Corp.

Riding Mountain National Park

Distance: 270 km (162 mi.)

Duration: 3–5 days

Rating: Strenuous

Type: Loop route

Access:

Located in a scenic valley, Minnedosa is 42 km (25 mi.) north of Brandon. Buses are available to Minnedosa.

Accommodations:

Full services are available at Brandon. Services are available at Minnedosa, Wasagaming, and Ste. Rose du Lac.

There are several campgrounds in Riding Mountain National Park. The Parks branch of the Department of Natural Resources will provide detailed information on campgrounds; phone (983) 945-3703.

Route Description:

Lying on the plateau of the Manitoba escarpment, and located 265 km (165 mi.) northwest of Winnipeg, Riding Mountain National Park is inhabited by a large variety of animal and bird life, including a herd of bison in an enclosure near Lake Audy. The park can be explored by a network of trails that are designed for hiking, cycling, and horseback riding. There is a resort town, Wasagaming, within the park, as well as a number of campgrounds and picnic areas. The Elkhorn Resort and Conference Centre, near Wasagaming, has chalets, a lodge, and a riding stable; even stagecoach rides are available.

Begin your tour at Minnedosa (located in a scenic valley), 42 km (25 mi.) north of Brandon. Take No. 10 north through Erickson to Wasagaming, a distance of 44 km (26 mi.); then cycle through Riding Mountain National Park. Ride on No. 10 and then No. 5, to 60 km (36 mi.) north of Wasagaming.

Turn east on No. 5 to Ste. Rose du Lac (known as the cattle capital of Manitoba), and then cycle south (still on No. 5) to

McCreary, on the eastern border of the park. Continue south to Norgate 42 km (25 mi.) south of Ste. Rose du Lac). Return to Riding Mountain National Park by turning west on No. 19, traveling 39 km (24 mi.) back to Wasagaming, on Clear Lake.

After you have explored the park, return to Minnedosa by cycling south on No. 10.

Most of the roads on this tour have relatively light traffic, but the terrain is hilly on the Escarpment.

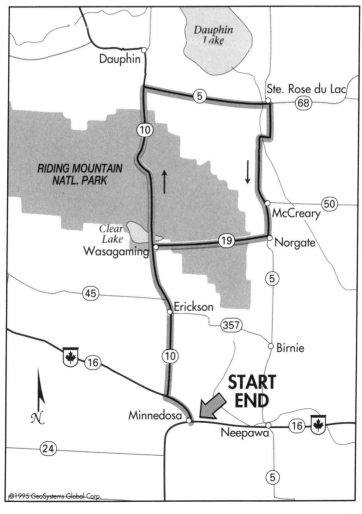

Ride to Dauphin:

A side trip of 10 km (6 mi.) north of the junction of No. 10 and No. 5 takes you to Dauphin, where full services are available. Near Dauphin, 12 km(8 mi.) south and 1 km (6 mi.) west of No. 10, is the Selo Ukraina, site of the Ukrainian Festival, held each August.

Ride to the Portia Marsh Interpretive Centre:

A side trip east from McCreary (on No. 50) to Alonsa (35 km (1 mi.) east of the park) gives you an opportunity to view wildlife. The Portia Marsh Interpretive Centre provides hiking on a boardwalk and on an upland trail.

Ride to Brandon:

Cycle south on No. 10 to Brandon, 42 km (25 mi.), Manitoba's second largest city. Here a paved bicycle path offers you interesting views of the city. You might like to visit such places of interest as the Brandon Research Station, the Commonwealth Air Training Plan Museum, and the Art Gallery of Southwestern Manitoba.

Optional Activities:

Riding Mountain National Park has a network of trails that are designed for hiking, cycling, or horseback riding.

For more information:

Riding Mountain National Park
Wasagaming, Manitoba R0J 2H0
Telephone (204) 848-2811.

Whiteshell Provincial Park

Distance: 210 km (126 mi.)

Duration: 2–4 days

Rating: Moderate

Type: Loop route

Access:

Falcon Lake is located about 140 km (84 mi.) east of Winnipeg. Buses are available.

Accommodations:

The resort town of Falcon Lake has services. There are several campgrounds, lodges, resorts, and marinas within the park. The Parks branch of the Department of Natural Resources will provide detailed information on campgrounds; phone (983) 945-3703.

Route Description:

One of Manitoba's largest parks, Whiteshell Provincial Park contains over 200 lakes and an abundance of fish (including perch, small-mouth bass, pike, walleye, and lake trout) and wildlife (including beaver, fox, deer, black bear, lynx, coyote, moose, turkey vulture, grouse, ruffed grouse, and bald eagle). The park is a popular area for canoeing and hiking; it is located near the Manitoba-Ontario border.

The rocks found in the park are part of the Precambrian Shield, the oldest geological formation in the world. Interesting hiking trails in the park include the 16 km (10 mi.) Hunt Lake Hiking Trail and the 60 km (36 mi.) Mantario Hiking Trail.

Begin your loop tour at Falcon Lake, on the Trans Canada Highway (near the Ontario border); a plaque commemorates the Old Dawson Trail. Cycle north on No. 312 to West Hawk Lake, the deepest in the province 111 m (365 ft.) and likely formed by a meteorite; this is a popular spot for scuba diving.

Continue northwest on No. 44 to Lily Pond, a water lily lake with cliffs composed of rocks billions of years old. Near

Rennie is the Alf Hole Goose Sanctuary, a nesting ground for Canada geese; a self-guided trail with interpretive signs rings the pond.

At Rennie, turn northwest on No. 307. At the northeastern tip of White Lake is Rainbow Falls, a picturesque spot for photographs. Near Betula Lake are the Bannock Point Petroforms, remains of ceremonial Ojibwa rock effigies. Just north of Betula Lake is another scenic spot for camera buffs: Pine Point Rapids. At Lake Nutimik, the Whiteshell Natural History Museum contains Indian artifacts, animals, and the ecology of Whiteshell Provincial Park.

Continue cycling on No. 307 to Seven Sisters Falls. Turn south on No. 408 and No. 44 to Whitemouth. Continue southeast on No. 44 to Rennie and then back to the starting point at Falcon Lake.

Many facilities are available in Whiteshell Provincial Park as you explore the beauty of this tranquil and fascinating area.

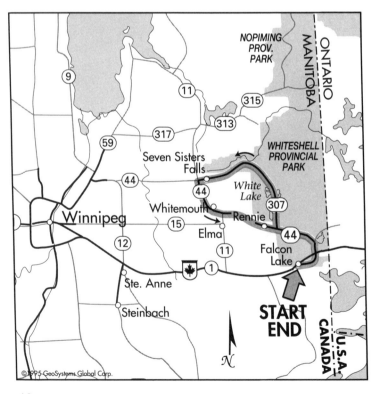

Ride to Lake Winnipeg beaches:

From Seven Sisters Falls, continue west on No. 307 to No. 11, and then cycle northwest on No. 11 to Belair, on Lake Winnipeg. Head south on No. 59 to Grand Beach Provincial Park, with its interpretive trails, campgrounds, white sand beaches, and magnificent sand dunes. Follow the shore of Lake Winnipeg by cycling south on No. 500 (unpaved). For information about Grand Beach Provincial Park, contact:
Grand Beach Provincial Park
Grand Beach, Manitoba R0E 0S0
Telephone (204) 754-2212.

Ride to Winnipeg:

Cycle west on No. 44 (from near Seven Sisters Falls) to Lockport. Then cycle south on No. 206 and west on No. 15 to Winnipeg, the capital of Manitoba.

Alternate: Continue the Lake Winnipeg beaches route (described above) by cycling southwest on No. 59, No. 508, No. 212, and No. 204 to Lower Fort Garry National Historic Park. Then continue riding on No. 204, along the Red River to Winnipeg (the route becomes No. 42 within the city).

These suggested routes to Winnipeg avoid the heavy traffic found on the Trans Canada Highway (No. 1), which does not have a paved shoulder in this section.

A Cyclist's Map of Winnipeg may be purchased from:
Canadian Cycling Association
1600 James Naismith Drive, Suite 810
Gloucester, Ontario K1B 5N4
Telephone (613) 748-5629
Fax (613) 748-5692

Maps can also be obtained from the Manitoba Cycling Association (address and phone number previously given) or from:
Winnipeg Cycletouring Club
Box 2068
Winnipeg, Manitoba R3C 3R4
Telephone (204) 772-4034

Ride to Birds Hill Provincial Park:

Birds Hill Provincial Park is the closest provincial park to Winnipeg. Hiking trails and campgrounds are found within this park. The 7 km (4.5 mi.) Pine Ridge Bicycle Trail takes you past pines and aspens as you circle the man-made lake.

An interesting loop tour of the park, from Winnipeg, is to cycle on No. 59 to No. 213; then take No. 213 east and No. 206 north to the east gate of the park. Ride through the park to the west gate, and then return on No. 59 (which has a wide paved shoulder) to Winnipeg. This loop is about 36 km (22 mi.) long.

Birds Hill Provincial Park can also be reached from the previously described optional trips. For example, if cycling to Winnipeg on No. 15, head north on No. 206 from Dugald to the east gate of the park. If cycling to Winnipeg from the Lake Winnipeg beaches option, ride south on No. 59 to the west gate of the park.

Optional Activities:

There are opportunities for fishing, canoeing, hiking, and scuba diving in Whiteshell Provincial Park. Hiking trails include the 16 km (10 mi.) Hunt Lake Hiking Trail and the 60 km (36 mi.) Mantario Hiking Trail. Scuba diving is most popular at deep West Hawk Lake.

Visit the Whiteshell Natural History Museum at Lake Nutimik, which contains Indian artifacts, animals, and information about the ecology of the park.

Visit the Alf Hole Goose Sanctuary (with a self-guided trail and interpretive signs) and the Bannock Point Petroforms.

For more information:

Tourism Winnipeg
232 - 375 York Ave.
Winnipeg, Manitoba R3C 3J
phone 1-800-665-0204

Chapter 7

New Brunswick

New Brunswick is home to such sights as the towering tides of the Bay of Fundy, the highest mountain in Atlantic Canada (in Mount Carleton Provincial Park), the Acadian Historical Village at Caraquet, the gorge at Grand Falls, the longest covered bridge at Hartland, and Magnetic Hill in Moncton.

With its vast network of picturesque roadways, New Brunswick is a very intriguing destination for the cyclist. The Trans Canada Highway, which crosses the province, has a wide paved shoulder; however, many of the less-traveled roads do not.

Average summer temperatures range from 13°C to 26°C (65°F to 78°F). It is of course cooler along the coast of the Bay of Fundy than in the interior.

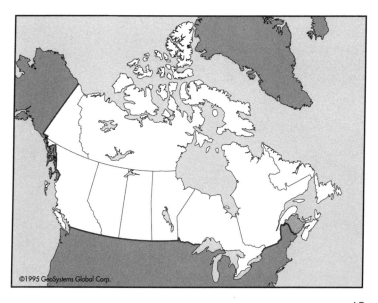

©1995 GeoSystems Global Corp.

A scene from Acadian Historical Village, near Caraquet, New Brunswick. (Photo courtesy New Brunswick Tourism)

For more information:

Canadian Hostelling
Association—New Brunswick
Box 6251, Station A,
St. John, N.B. E2L 4R7.

New Brunswick Cycling
Association
114 Morton Ave.
Moncton, N.B. E1A 3H6
Telephone (506) 854-8876

Tourism New Brunswick
P.O. Box 12345
Fredericton, N.B. E3B 5C
Telephone 1-800-442-4442 (in
N.B.); 1-800-561-0123 (from
outside N.B.)
(Vacation guides and
self-escorted bicycle tours are
available)

The Isles of Fundy

Distance: 225 km (135 mi.)

Duration: 3–5 days

Rating: easy/moderate

Type: return trip

Access:

Located in the southwest coastal area of New Brunswick, St. Andrews is a lovely seaside resort. St. Andrews is 100 km (60 mi.) west of St. John

Accommodations:

Full services are available at St. Andrews and on the islands.

Route Description:

Situated in the western extremity of the Bay of Fundy are a lovely trio of islands, worthy of exploration: Deer, Campobello, and Grand Manan.

Begin your tour in the lovely coastal town of St. Andrews, where the many historic buildings add distinction. You may wish to visit Ross Memorial Museum, the Huntsman Marine Science Centre and Aquarium (which provides information about the Bay of Fundy), and St. Andrews Blockhouse National Historic Site.

Take No. 127 north through the rolling countryside, with views of the sea and the fishing boats. Turn east on No. 1 at Digdeguash to St. George (where a monster supposedly lives in Lake Utopia). Visit beautiful Magaguadavic Falls and watch the salmon jumping the rapids on their journey upriver to spawn. The Protestant Cemetery, to St. Mark's Anglican Church, is one of the oldest in Canada; the country's oldest Presbyterian church is also located in St. George.

Cycle south on No. 43 to Letete, 45 km (27 mi.) from St. Andrews. Take the ferry from Letete to Deer Island, which lies at the entrance to Passamaquoddy Bay.

Surrounded by a mosaic of smaller islands, Deer Island provides many opportunities for whale watching, bird watching, rockhounding, scuba diving, cycling, and hiking. Offshore is Old Sow, the second largest whirlpool in the world.

A toll ferry takes you from Deer Island to Campobello Island. Campobello can also be reached by an international bridge, the Franklin D. Roosevelt Memorial Bridge, from Lubec, Maine.

Former U.S. President Franklin Delano Roosevelt, who spent several summers here, called Campobello Island the Beloved Isle. Roosevelt International Park features the president's 34-room cottage, complete with childhood photos and sketches.

Herring Cove Provincial Park, on Campobello Island, has camping facilities and a long stretch of pebbly beach. Strategically located lighthouses add a distinctive beauty to

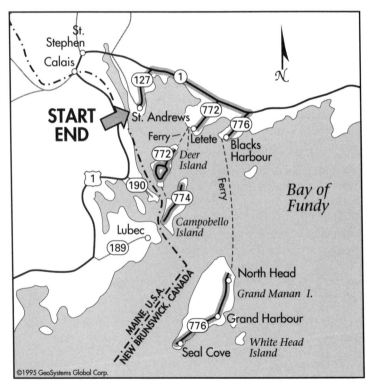

the shoreline as they guide ships through treacherous passages.

After exploring Campobello and Deer Islands, return by ferry to the mainland, and cycle north on No. 43 to St. George. Turn east on No. 1 to Pennfield, and turn south on No. 776 to Blacks Harbour, an important fish-processing center and the site of the North American Sardine Packing Championships.

Take the 2-hour ferry ride from Blacks Harbour to Grand Manan Island, the largest and most remote of the three Fundy Isles.

James Audubon, the renowned ornithologist, did many of his sketches on Grand Manan Island, a birdwatcher's paradise; more than 250 species of birds have been sighted. Whale watching, rockhounding, painting, photography, hiking, and cycling are other popular activities.

You will arrive by ferry at North Head. Take the main road, which runs along the sea for 29 km (18 mi.) through quaint villages (Castalia, Grand Harbour, Seal Cove) and past magnificent seascapes. Near Seal Cove you will find Anchorage Provincial Park and a bird sanctuary. If you wish, you can take another ferry to White Head Island.
The eastern side of Grand Manan Island has long, sandy beaches and a number of small villages; the western side is characterized by seaweed and high cliffs. Most of North America's dulce, an edible seaweed, is harvested from this island. Grand Manan Island is 35 km (21 mi.) long and up to 10 km (6 mi.) wide.

Return to North Head and take the ferry back to the mainland. Cycle north on No. 776 back to Pennfield, and then ride west on No. 1 and south on No. 127 to the completion of this tour at St. Andrews.

Ride into Maine:

Cross the Franklin D. Roosevelt Memorial Bridge from Campobello Island, New Brunswick, to Lubec, Maine (in the U.S.), and then begin a tour of Maine.

Ride to St. John:

After exploring Grand Manan Island and returning to Pennfield on the mainland, turn east on No. 1 (the Trans

Canada Highway, with its wide paved shoulder), and cycle about 60 km (36 mi.) to St. John, Canada's oldest incorporated city. Rockwood Park, in the heart of the city, is a good place from which to get a view of the Reversing Falls. This is where the high tides of the Bay of Fundy cause the St. John River to flow in the opposite direction, a twice-daily occurance).

Optional Activities:

Hike the Sunbury Shores Nature Trail at St. Andrews.

St. Andrews Scuba Club offers diving packages. Scuba diving services are also found on the islands.

Rockhounding.

Bird-watching and fishing trips.

Whale-watching trips are available on all three islands and at St. Andrews.

Several hiking trails exist in Herring Cove Provincial Park and Roosevelt Campobello International Park, both found on Campobello Island. There is also a coastal trail in Anchorage Provincial Park and 70 km (42 mi.) of other trails on Grand Manan Island. A trail guide may be purchased from:
Grand Manan Museum
Grand Harbour, N.B. E0G 1X0

For more information:

St. Andrews Chamber of Commerce
P.O. Box 89
St. Andrews By-the-Sea, N.B. E0G 2X0
Telephone (506) 529-3000

Superintendent, Anchorage Provincial Park
Seal Cove
Grand Manan Island, N.B. E0G 3B0
Telephone (506) 662-3215

For Grand Manan Island ferry service:
Coastal Transportation Ltd.
Box 26
St. John, N.B. E2L 3X1
Telephone (506) 657-3306

Fundy Tidal Trail

Distance: 215 km (108 mi.)

Duration: 2–3 days

Rating: Moderate

Type: Loop route

Access:

Moncton has a comfortable blend of French and English culture, and it is the major center of the Southeast Shores Tourist Area of New Brunswick. Moncton has both rail and airport facilities.

Accommodations:

Full services are available in Moncton and Alma. There are several bed-and-breakfasts in the Hopewell Cape area. Accommodations abound in Fundy National Park, from backcountry campsites to housekeeping chalets.

Route Description:

From charming inland communities to bustling fishing villages, from Magnetic Hill to stunning seascapes, from blueberries and rolling countryside to tide-worn rocks and high tides, the Fundy Tidal Trail has a variety of splendors for you.

Begin your tour in the city of Moncton, New Brunswick's second largest city, where you can visit the Moncton Museum, Acadian Museum, and Centennial Park. Magnetic Hill lets you test the law of gravity, as you seem to coast uphill.

Cycle south from Moncton on No. 114 (the Fundy Tidal Trail), and follow the Petitcodiac River to Hillsborough, where clapboard houses along the waterfront evoke images of earlier times.

Continue your ride to Hopewell Cape, site of Rocks Provincial Park, one of the most photographed attractions in eastern Canada. Here, tides have carved the Flower Pot Rocks. At high tide, these rocks look like small islands; at low tide, you can walk on the beach among them. The rock formations stand as a testament to the strength of the mighty Fundy tides, the highest in the world.

The Albert County Museum is housed in the former county jail in Hopewell Cape; antiques, quilts, tools, and exhibits on the history of sailing are displayed.

Leaving Hopewell Cape, travel southwest on No. 114 to Riverside-Albert and Alma (at the edge of Fundy National Park). Alma is a service area for visitors to the park. You can also walk on the ocean floor at Alma at low tide.

Overlooking the Bay of Fundy, Fundy National Park is a wildlife sanctuary and recreation area; it is characterized by meadows of wildflowers, rushing waterfalls, placid lakes, majestic cliffs, an abundance of wildlife, and the awesome tides. A bowling green, tennis courts, and a golf course are available in the park. Salt water is piped in from the Bay of Fundy and heated for the swimming pool in Fundy National Park.

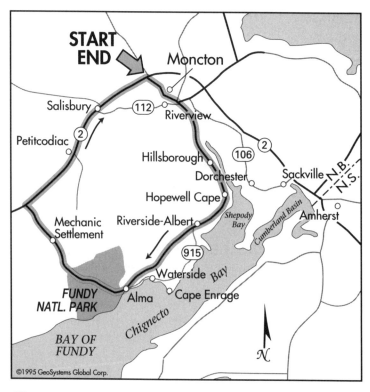

Cycle on No. 114 northwest through the park. Continue through Mechanic Settlement to the junction of No. 114 and No. 2 (the Trans Canada Highway). Turn northeast on No. 2, and cycle on the wide paved shoulder to Petitcodiac (near here a collection of over 2,000 dolls is displayed at Delia's Dollhouse) and then back to Moncton.

Ride to Sussex:

When you reach the Trans Canada Highway, cycle west to Sussex, an important dairy, poultry, and crafts center. Sussex was founded by Loyalists in 1786. It's the site of an annual hot air balloon festival. Sussex is only 75 km (45 mi.) west of Moncton, so this trip would add on about 30 km (18 mi.) to the detailed tour.

Optional Activities:

Walk on the ocean floor at low tide.

Bird watch, cycle, hike, fish, beachcomb, boat, golf, lawn bowl, play tennis, swim, or participate in a nature interpretive program in Fundy National Park.

Hiking trails in Fundy National Park range from short boardwalks to treks to overnight backcountry campsites; the trails lead to old farms, swimming holes, waterfalls, and coastal panoramas.

Beaches in Fundy National Park include Alma, Herring, and Point Wolfe.

For more information:

Fundy National Park
P.O. Box 40
Alma, N.B. E0A 1B0
Telephone (506) 887-2000

Bathurst to Kouchibouguac National Park

Distance: 267 km (160 mi.)

Duration: 3–6 days

Rating: easy / moderate

Type: one-way tour

Access:

Bathurst is located on the northeastern coast of New Brunswick, at the mouth of the Nepisiguit River (Micmac for "tumultuous river"). It is the only city on the Acadian Trail, and it boasts the largest zinc mines in North America.

This one-way tour ends in Kouchibouguac National Park. At Kouchibouguac, you rejoin No. 11; you may cycle south on No. 11 and No. 15 to Moncton (108 km / 65 mi.) or northwest on No. 11 and No. 8 back to Bathurst (117 km / 70 mi.).

Accommodations:

Full services are available at Bathurst and Chatham. Several campgrounds and bed-and-breakfast inns are found along this route. Campgrounds are also available in Kouchibouguac National Park.

Route Description:

You will follow along the Acadian coast as you cycle from Bathurst to Kouchibouguac National Park on this scenic tour.

Begin your trip in Bathurst, located at the mouth of the Nepisiguit River on Bathurst Harbour in northeastern New Brunswick. Cycle northeast on No. 11, along the Baie des Chaleurs, to Salmon Beach, Janeville, Stonehaven, Pokeshaw (Pokeshaw Rock is a haven for many species of birds), and Grand-Anse, where you can buy fresh fish at the public wharf.

Cycle to Bertrand and Caraquet. Caraquet is considered to be the cultural capital of Acadia, and an Acadian Festival is held here each August. The Acadian Museum, in Caraquet, portrays the history of the local people.

Thousands of people make a religious pilgrimage each year to the Sainte-Anne-du-Bocage Shrine, near Caraquet. The shrine was founded in memory of the area's settlers. Also nearby is the Acadian Historical Village, which re-creates the lives of Acadians between 1780 and 1890. Acadian dishes can be sampled at the village's restaurant.

After exploring the area around Caraquet, continue cycling to Tracadie, Rivière-du-Portage, Wishart Point, Negauc, and Chatham. You will pass several beaches on this route.

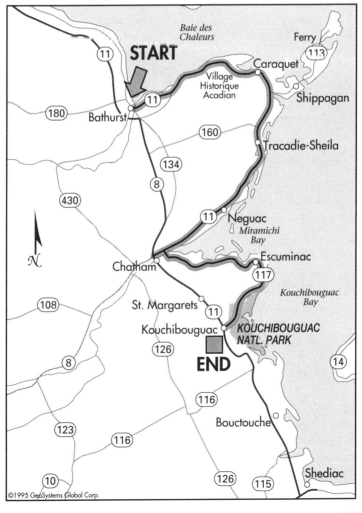

Located on Miramichi Bay, Chatham has such points of interest as Rankin House (a restored 19th-century Georgian mansion), W. S. Loggie Cultural Centre, St. Michael's Historical Museum, Miramichi Natural History Museum, and MacDonald Farm Historic Park.

Leaving Chatham, follow No. 117 along Miramichi Bay to Escuminac. Then cycle southwest along the Gulf of St. Lawrence and into Kouchibouguac National Park. Cycle through the park to the village of Kouchibouguac, the destination of this beautiful trip.

Kouchibouguac National Park offers 30 km (18 mi.) of paved cycling paths (there are even some campsites on the route). There is also a network of trails in the park for the avid mountain biker and hiker. Enjoy the sand dunes, beaches, salt marshes, bogs, lagoons, and forests of this wilderness and wetlands area in the heart of Acadia. There are several species of orchids in the park. Many migratory birds visit the area. Wildlife in the park includes beaver, deer, black bear, moose, fox, and coyote. Harbor seals are found along the coast.

Bathurst Loop Tour by Bicycle:

Cycle northwest on No. 11 from Kouchibouguac to Chatham. Then ride north on No. 8 back to Bathurst. This additional 117 km (70 mi.) makes the detailed tour into a loop tour.

Ride to Mount Carleton Provincial Park:

Cycle west on No. 180 from Bathurst (which becomes a gravel road), and then ride southeast into the park. The highest mountain in Atlantic Canada is found in Mount Carleton Provincial Park. This wilderness park offers camping, boating, swimming, and hiking.

Ride to Moncton:

Cycle southeast on No. 11 from Kouchibouguac to Shediac, called the lobster capital of the world. Then ride southwest on No. 15 (with a wide paved shoulder) to Moncton, the capital of New Brunswick. This trip from Kouchibouguac to Moncton is 108 km (65 mi.) long.

Ride to Miscou Island:

A side trip in the northeast corner of New Brunswick is to cycle on No. 113 north through Shippagon (an important commercial shipping center) and across the causeway to Ile Lamèque. You will view the peat bogs as you ride on this island. You may decide to stop at Le Paradis des Animaux, a wildlife park, or visit the distinctive Ste.-Cecile Church, with its native art and excellent acoustics (it hosts an international festival of baroque music). Then take the ferry to the remote, sparsely populated Miscou Island. While on this island, you can cycle the 18 km (11 mi.) main route and explore the long stretches of sandy beaches. Saltwater bass fishing is available, or you can take a deep-sea fishing excursion.

Cycle Quebec's Gaspé Peninsula:

For a challenging extended trip, you can cycle northwest (on No. 11) from Bathurst to Campbellton, and cross the bridge into the province of Quebec. Then cycle on No. 132 around the Gaspé Peninsula, a spectacular but strenuous route (a total of 1,130 km/678 mi.] back to Bathurst).

The route is mountainous, with several panoramic ocean views; the roads have unpaved shoulders for most of this trip, and tourist traffic can be rather heavy.

Ride west to Matapedia and then northwest to Mont-Joli. Then follow the rugged coastline as you cycle around the peninsula, visiting such places of interest as Matane, known for its shrimp and salmon; Les Méchins, where the streets are named after fishermen's boats; Sainte-Anne-des-Monts, a ski resort; Mont-Saint-Pierre, with its panoramic view and glider launching pads; Grande-Vallée, with its covered bridge; Forillon National Park, where harbor seals and whales can be viewed from high limestone cliffs; Gaspé, where a monument commemorates the landing of the French explorer Jacques Cartier; Percé, with its often photographed Perce Rock; L'Anse-aux-Gascons, with its white sand beach; Bonaventure, an Acadian farming center; and Saint-Omer, famous for its clam-digging.

Complete your loop on Quebec's Gaspé Peninsula, and then cycle back to Bathurst, New Brunswick.

Optional Activities:

There is an easy 3 km (2 mi.) walking loop in Val Comeau Provincial Park.

A narrow sandspit extending well out into the Baie de Caraquet provides an easy walking trip in Maisonnette Beach Provincial Park, with opportunities to view shorebirds and the salt marshes.

Kayak or sail on the Baie des Chaleurs.

Visit the Sainte-Anne-du-Bocage Shrine and Acadian Historical Village, near Caraquet.

Kouchibouguac National Park has both interpretive trails and hiking trails for hikers and backpackers. The park also provides paved bike paths and mountain bike trails. Anglers need a license to fish for the flounder, smelt, trout, and striped bass.

For more information:

Forillon National Park
P.O. Box 1220
Gaspé, Quebec G0C 1R0
Telephone (418) 368-5505

Gaspé Tourism Association
357 route de la Mer
Ste.-Flavie, Quebec G0J 2L0
Telephone (418) 775-2223

Kouchibouguac National Park
Kouchibouguac,
N.B. E0A 2A0
Telephone (506) 876-2443

Chapter 8

Newfoundland

Newfoundland, Canada's youngest province, is a rugged, rocky island off the eastern coast of Canada's mainland. The rugged terrain, along with the warmth and wit of its inhabitants, make Newfoundland an exciting and friendly destination for cyclists.

The coastline provides many challenging rides on narrow roads; however, the relatively traffic-free environment adds to your tranquility. Be prepared, though, as you may cycle in areas that offer very few services. You may also encounter strong winds and fog along the coast.

The major highway across the province, the Trans Canada Highway (No. 1), offers you a wide paved shoulder and more traffic.

Summer days in Newfoundland range from cool to hot, with an average temperature of 16°C (61°F). Be prepared for temperature changes, and bring rain gear.

This chapter comprises descriptions of 2 different tours.

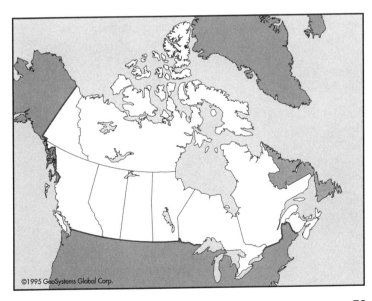

©1995 GeoSystems Global Corp.

Brigus South, on Conception Bay. (Photo courtesy J. Byrne, Dept. of Tourism and Culture, Newfoundland and Labrador)

For more information:

Department of Tourism and Culture
P.O. Box 8730
St. John's, Nfld. A1C 5R8
Telephone 1-800-563-6353

Hostelling International Newfoundland
P.O. Box 1815
St. John's, Nfld. A1C 5P9
Telephone (709) 739-5866

The Newfoundland and Labrador Cycling Association
Box 2127, Station C
St. John's, Nfld. A1C 5R6
Telephone (709) 576-2513

Marine Atlantic Coastal Ferries
P.O. Box 250
North Sydney N.S. B2A 3M3
Telephone (902) 794-5700 (from North Sydney, N.S.); (709) 772-7701 (from St. John's, Nfld.); (709) 695-7081 (from Channel Port-aux Basques, Nfld.); 1-800-341-7981 (from Bar Harbor, Maine)

Gros Morne National Park

Distance: 200 km (120 mi.)

Duration: 2–4 days

Rating: Strenuous

Type: Return trip

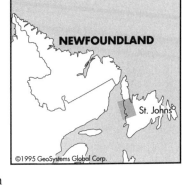

Access:

Deer Lake has air service and is located on the Trans Canada Highway, at the junction of No. 430 (which takes you north into Gros Morne National Park). Bus service is also available.

Accommodations:

Several services are available in Deer Lake, but this trip into the park is most suitable for campers.

Route Description:

The most spectacular section of the Long Range Mountains is found on Newfoundland's west coast in Gros Morne National Park. Glacial erosion sculpted the park into its present grandeur. You cycle through wilderness, past lakes, and have many striking views of fjords, high cliffs, and other natural marvels. You pass some sandy beaches, but much of the shoreline is rugged and covered with boulders. Barnacles, sea urchins, hermit crabs, mussels, and starfish are among the sea life to be found in the coastal tidal pools.

Begin this challenging trip at Deer Lake, 50 km (30 mi.) east of Corner Brook. Cycle north on No. 430, the Viking Trail, for 23 km (14 mi.) to Wiltondale, where you will find an interesting museum, as well as the entrance to Gros Morne National Park, designated as a World Heritage Site in 1987.

Ride into the park (on No. 430) to Rocky Harbour, on Bonne Bay, the headquarters of the park. Bonne Bay is known for its picturesque fjords and schools of mackerel. The Lomond River, off the east arm of Bonne Bay, is a good place to fish for Atlantic salmon.

Continue cycling in the park to Green Point, where there is a campground near the ocean; Sally Cove, a popular area for

81

lobster fishing; Western Brook Pond, a spectacular inland fjord between high cliffs; St. Paul's Inlet; Cow Head, with its great views of the coast of the Gulf of St. Lawrence and its driftwood-strewn beach; and on to the northern tip of Gros Morne National Park.

After you have cycled to the north end of the park, simply reverse directions; continue to explore this fascinating park as you ride back (still on No. 430). The traffic should be relatively light as you cycle, on a paved road, through this challenging but spectacular area.

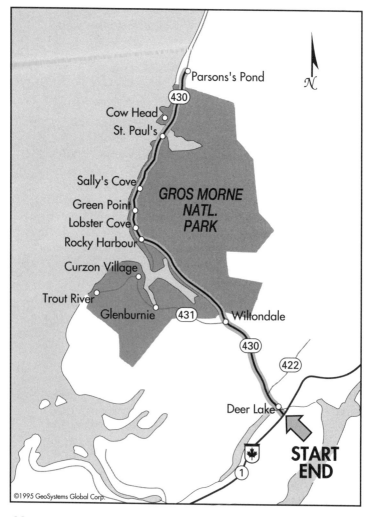

Newfoundland's moose population is among the densest in the world, so be on the lookout for these great animals, weighing up to 544 kg (1,200 lbs) as you cycle through the park. Black bears are also quite plentiful.

You eventually exit from the southern part of the park. Cycle back to Deer Lake to complete this tour.

Ride to Labrador:

If you want to extend your trip by several days, exit from the north end of the park and continue cycling on the Viking Trail (No. 430) to St. Barbe, near the northern tip of Newfoundland. From here you can take a ferry across the Strait of Belle Isle to Blanc Sablon, on the Quebec-Labrador border. You can then explore a part of Labrador by cycling northeast on No. 510, a paved road, to Pinware River Provincial Park (camping available) and on to Red Bay.

This is a good area for bird watching, whale watching and viewing icebergs. The largest caribou herd in the world resides in Labrador.

At Red Bay, you can return to Newfoundland by ferry, arriving at St. Anthony. You can then visit the World Heritage Site of L'Anse aux Meadows by cycling north on No. 430 and then on an unpaved road, No. 436. It is believed that Vikings visited this area as early as the 11th century, establishing the first European settlement in North America.

You can also take a ferry from St. Anthony to Lewisporte.

Optional Activities:

Fishing for Atlantic salmon.

Take a tour boat at Western Brook Pond to enjoy the picturesque fjords. You will pass high cliffs and spectacular waterfalls.

There are several hiking trails within Gros Morne National Park, including:
> the Tablelands (a flat section in the southern part of the park)
> the James Callaghan Loop Trail to the top of Gros Morne (the mountain that gave the park its name).

For more information:

For information on ferries between Labrador and Newfoundland, phone 1-800-563-7336.

For information on the St. Barbe–Blanc Sablon ferry service, phone (709) 722-4000.

Superintendent, Gros Morne National Park
P.O. Box 130
Rocky Harbour, Nfld. A0K 4N0
Telephone (709) 458-2417

Avalon Peninsula and Conception Bay

Distance: 170 km (102 mi.)

Duration: 2–3 days

Rating: Strenuous

Type: One-way tour

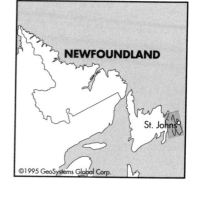

Access:

A ferry from the mainland makes Newfoundland accessible by motor vehicle and bicycle. The ferry docks at Argentia, on the Avalon Peninsula. Air service is available from St. John's, this tour's destination. St. John's is the traditional beginning and ending city on a tour across Canada.

Accommodations:

There are several bed-and-breakfast inns and camping areas along this route. Full services are available in St. John's.

Route Description:

When you arrive at Argentia, Newfoundland, from Canada's mainland, you cycle on the Avalon Peninsula. This trip takes you along a section of this interesting peninsula and around beautiful Conception Bay as you ride from the ferry dock to St. John's. West of the capital city of St. John's is the picturesque Conception Bay area, with its tiny fishing villages and sheltered harbors.

Your route begins at the ferry dock at Argentia. Ride along the Avalon Peninsula as you follow No. 100 to No. 1 (the Trans Canada Highway). Go east on No. 1 to No. 73, and then cycle north along Trinity Bay's shoreline, through Backside Pond (camping available), Cavendish, Hearts Delight, Hearts Desire, and on to Hearts Content (site of the first successful trans-Atlantic telegraphic communication), 75 km (45 mi.) from Argentia.

Take No. 74 from Hearts Content, cycling southeast, and descend into Carboneau. Go south on No. 70 to Harbour Grace (location of Newfoundland's oldest stone church) and

Bay Roberts. This hilly road offers you many views of beautiful Conception Bay from the western shoreline. Take No. 70 and then No. 60 along the rugged coastline to Cupids, Brigus, Georgetown, Conception Harbour, Avondale, Harbour Main, and Holyrood (site of Butter Pot Provincial Park).

Having rounded the tip of the bay, cycle north on No. 60 along the eastern shore of Conception Bay, passing Seal Cove, Kelligrews (celebrated in the ballad "The Kelligrew Soiree"), Foxtrap, and into Topsail. The pavement is rough in spots,

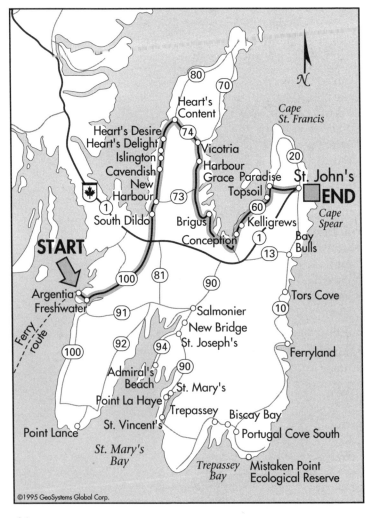

©1995 GeoSystems Global Corp.

and the traffic can be heavy as you cycle along Conception Bay. This section of the trip is, however, relatively level.

Ride east from Topsail to St. John's, the end of this scenic tour on the Avalon Peninsula and around Conception Bay.

From the top of Signal Hill (in St. John's), you can view the city and the coastline.

Ride to Cape Spear:

Cycle east from St. John's on No. 11 to Cape Spear 10 km (6 mi.). This is the easternmost point on the Avalon Peninsula and as far east as you can go in North America.

Avalon Peninsula loop cycling tour:

You may complete a loop back to Argentia by cycling along the east coast of the Avalon Peninsula (on No. 10) from St. John's to St. Vincent's. Follow No. 90 north to Salmonier. Take No. 91 west to Freshwater, and then return to Argentia. This trip on the peninsula will have little traffic or services as you cycle in hilly terrain (particularly from Trepassey to St. Vincent's) and follow the rugged, picturesque coastline of southeastern Newfoundland.

Visit St. Pierre and Miquelon:

For an extended trip, you could cycle west from St. John's on No. 1 to Goobies and southwest on No. 210 to Winterland. Then ride to Frenchman's Cove and down the Burin Peninsula to Fortune. From Fortune, you can take a 2-hour ferry ride to the French islands of St. Pierre and Miquelon, where you can explore a part of France. This trip is 350 km (210 mi.) in length; you cycle on paved roads and on rolling terrain.

For information on the ferry between Fortune and St. Pierre, contact:

Lake and Lake Ltd.
P.O. Box 98
Fortune, Nfld. A0E 1P0
Telephone (709) 832-0429 or
(709) 738-1357 (from St. John's)

Optional Activities:

Fishing in the streams for salmon and trout.

Deep-sea fishing for bluefin tuna in Conception Bay.

South of St. John's you can take a boat tour to islands with great seabird colonies. Gull, Green, and Great Islands are bird sanctuaries off the east coast of the Avalon Peninsula. This area boasts one of the largest puffin colonies on the east coast of North America.

Whale-watching and bird-watching charters to Gull Island are available from Bay Bulls.

For more information:

Phone the St. John's Tourist Commission Office at (709) 722-7080.

Chapter 9

Nova Scotia

From St. Ann's Gaelic College (on the Cabot Trail), the only school of its kind in North America, to the tartaned pipers who reside in the province, Nova Scotia (New Scotland) is never far from its origins.

Connected to the rest of the mainland by the isthmus of Chignecto, Nova Scotia includes the adjoining Cape Breton Island. The Trans Canada Highway (with its wide paved shoulder) stretches across the province from Amherst to Sydney. The southern coastline of the province and the northern section of Cape Breton Island are particularly hilly.

Sea breezes keep summer temperatures averaging about 21°C (70°F). At times you may encounter rain and fog, so be prepared.

In this chapter, 3 different routes are described, ranging from 1 to 5 days.

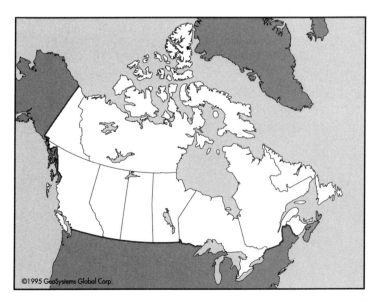

©1995 GeoSystems Global Corp.

Peggy's Cove lighthouse, Nova Scotia. (Photo courtesy Tourism Nova Scotia)

For More Information:

Bicycle Nova Scotia
Box 3010
South Halifax, N.S. B3J 3G6
Telephone (902) 425-5450

Canadian Hostelling
Association
5516 Spring Garden Road
Box 3010
South Halifax, N.S. B3J 3T3
Telephone (902) 425-5450

Interprovince ferry
information:
Telephone:
1-800-565-9411 (in Canada)
1-800-341-7981 (in U.S.)

Nova Scotia Tourism and
Culture
P.O. Box 130
Halifax, N.S. B3J 2M7
Telephone:
1-800-565-0000 (in Canada);
1-800-341-6096 (in U.S.)

Peggy's Cove

Distance: 110 km (66 mi.)

Duration: 1–2 days

Rating: moderate

Type: loop route

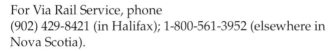

Access:

There is an international airport at Halifax.

For Via Rail Service, phone (902) 429-8421 (in Halifax); 1-800-561-3952 (elsewhere in Nova Scotia).

Acadian Bus Lines serves most of the larger towns and will carry bicycles if there is room. Contact: Acadian Bus Lines, 6040 Almon St., Halifax, Nova Scotia B3K 1&8; telephone (902) 454-9321.

Accommodations:

A wide range of accommodations, including bed-and-breakfast inns, camping, hostels, and luxury hotels, are available in the Halifax area. Services are also available along this route.

Route Description:

The old lighthouse on a massive granite ledge and fishing boats along weather-worn wharves have made this a very popular area for photographers and artists. Peggy's Cove is one of several fishing villages built around the snug harbors of the south coast of Nova Scotia. This loop tour will take you through hilly terrain, past many picturesque fishing villages along the shore of the Atlantic Ocean.

Begin this tour from Halifax, the capital of Nova Scotia. Halifax Citadel National Historic Park sits on a hill overlooking downtown Halifax. Other points of interest in Halifax include the Chapel of Our Lady of Sorrows, Old Dutch Church, St. Paul's Church, St. George's Round Church, the Art Gallery of Nova Scotia, Nova Scotia Museum, Maritime Museum of the Atlantic, Province House, York Redoubt National Historic Site, and Point Pleasant Park.

Take No. 333 south from Halifax to Goodwood, Whites Lake, Shad Bay, and Peggy's Cove (45 km/27 mi. from Halifax). Enjoy the charm of this tiny village, and then continue on this route through Glen Margaret and Seabright to Upper Tentallon. Then cycle on No. 3 east to Five Island Lake, Timberlea, and back to Halifax.

Halifax-Dartmouth Bridges:

There is no cycling across the bridges between Halifax and Dartmouth. However, you are allowed to walk your bicycle across the Angus L. MacDonald Bridge. You may also take your bicycle on the ferry between Halifax and Dartmouth during the weekdays.

Ride to Lunenburg:

Instead of returning directly to Halifax, you can extend your trip and see more of the coastal area by cycling west on No. 1 around Margarets Bay and Mahone Bay to Lunenburg, one of

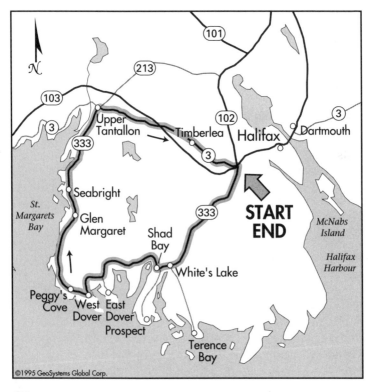

the greatest fishing ports on the continent. Located on a peninsula, Lunenburg is the site of some of Canada's oldest churches. Tours of the harbor are available aboard a Lunenburg-built schooner.

On this side trip, you will pass Graves Island Provincial Park, on the shore of Mahone Bay, and Chester, where you can take boat trips to the Tancook Islands in Mahone Bay.

Ride around the Minas Basin:

Take No. 2 from Halifax to Truro, where you can enjoy the hiking trails and waterfalls in Victoria Park. Then continue cycling on No. 2, along the Minas Basin. You will pass Great Village, where several 19th-century sea captains' mansions are on display, and climb Economy Mountain for a panoramic view of the area on your way to Five Islands Provincial Park, with its view of the five offshore islands.

Continue cycling west to Parrsboro, the largest town on the northern shore of the Minas Basin—and a good area for rockhounding. A short trip south will provide you with a view of a picturesque lighthouse (Partridge Island). This route has some hills but is not particularly difficult. Traffic is relatively light. There is not a paved shoulder for most of this trip.

Optional Activities:

Visit Halifax Citadel, one of the best surviving examples of 19th-century fortifications in Canada.

Sightseeing tours of Halifax and the harbor area are available.

The Evangeline Trail

Distance: 225 km (135 mi.)

Duration: 3–4 days

Rating: moderate

Type: one-way tour

©1995 GeoSystems Global Corp.

Access:

Grand Pré is located on the southern shore of the Minas Basin, just west of the Avon River (about 90 km/54 mi.) northwest of Halifax). Buses are available.

Your destination is Digby Neck, the peninsula that juts out into the Bay of Fundy, southwest of Digby. Buses are available at Digby; there is also ferry service to St. John, New Brunswick.

Accommodations:

Services are available in Wolfville, Middleton, Bridgetown, Annapolis Royal, and Digby. There are several bed-and-breakfast inns and camping facilities along this route.

Route Description:

This tour of the land of Longfellow's poetic heroine Evangeline takes you on a ride along the Atlantic seaboard, through an area of historical significance, past rocky headlands, picturesque fishing villages, and fragrant orchards, traveling on quiet, paved country roads with hilly terrain.

Begin this trip in Grand Pré, where Grand Pré National Historic Park commemorates the British expulsion of the Acadians in 1755, an event that was recorded in Longfellow's poem *Evangeline*.

Take No. 1 west to Wolfville, which was resettled by New Englanders after the expulsion of the Acadians. You have quite an easy ride through a trellis of dykes built by the French Acadians over 300 years ago to protect the flat farmland of the Minas Basin; these dykes hold back the tides of the Bay of Fundy.

Take No. 358 north from Wolfville to Canning, at the east end of the Annapolis Valley. Take No. 221 west from Canning to Middleton (site of Annapolis Valley MacDonald Museum), and then cycle on the Clarence Road along the base of the North Mountain to Bridgetown. Above Bridgetown is Valleyview Provincial Park, which provides a panoramic view of the Annapolis Valley.

The Annapolis Valley is Nova Scotia's famous fruit-growing area. It's protected by mountains. You can stop to purchase (in season) blueberries, raspberries, plums, apples, cherries, or strawberries.

Cycle west on No. 1 from Bridgetown to Annapolis Royal, which served as the capital of Nova Scotia from 1710 until the founding of Halifax in 1749. Annapolis Royal is the location of Fort Anne National Historic Park and Museum; Fort Anne was originally built by the French in the 1630s.

Cycle from Annapolis Royal to Port Royal, where you can visit Port Royal Habitation National Historic Park, which is a restoration of the original Port Royal, North America's oldest white settlement.

After exploring these historical sites, cycle over North Mountain and leave the rich farmland of the Annapolis Valley as you ride west on No. 1 to Digby, which overlooks the Annapolis Basin and Digby Gap (a great view). Digby is famous for its smoked herring, called Digby Chicken, and its scallops.

Leaving Digby, head down the slender peninsula of Digby Neck on No. 217, passing fishing hamlets with lobster traps piled on the docks. Digby Neck is on the Atlantic Flyway for migratory birds, so it is an excellent area for viewing osprey, puffins, great blue herons, cormorants, and razorbills.

Sandy Cove, 37 km (22 mi.) from Digby, is a paradise for rock hounds (agate, amethyst, jasper). Long Island, 34 km (21 mi.) west of Sandy Cove, is a good spot to take a whale-watching cruise on the Bay of Fundy; watch for finback, minke, and humpback whales, as well as for dolphins.

Side trip to Cape Blomidon:

When you arrive at Canning on the detailed tour, continue north on No. 358 to the village of The Lookoff, where you will find a magnificent view of the Minas Basin, with its red mud flats and the Annapolis Valley, with its bountiful orchards. Continue cycling north to Scots Bay. There is a 13 km (8 mi.) hiking trail to a spectacular lookout at Cape Split, known for its tides, winds, and seabirds.

Ride to Brier Island:

From Freeport, Long Island, on Digby Neck, you can take a ferry to Westport, Brier Island. You can then cycle to the westernmost tip of the peninsula. There is a paved road.

You can take a 72 km (43 mi.) ferry ride from Digby, Nova Scotia, to St. John, New Brunswick. Daily service. Reservations required; phone 1-800-565-9470.

Side Trip to Kejimkujik National Park:

Take No. 8 southeast from Annapolis Royal to Maitland Bridge. Enter Kejimkujik National Park, where canoes, rowboats, and bikes can be rented during the summer. Canoe routes, hiking trails, and backcountry campsites are available. The park is about 55 km (33 mi.) from Annapolis Royal.

Ride to Yarmouth:

You can cycle southwest on No. 101 and No. 1 from Digby to Yarmouth (about 85 km/51 mi.). From Yarmouth, you can take a ferry to either Bar Harbor or Portland, Maine.

Optional Activities:

Whale-watching cruises and fishing charters on the Bay of Fundy are available.

For more information:

Superintendent
Kejimkujik National Park
Box 36
Maitland Bridge, Annapolis
County, Nova Scotia B0T 1N0
Telephone (902) 242-2772.

The Cabot Trail

Distance: 295 km (177 mi.)

Duration: 3–5 days

Rating: strenuous

Type: loop route

©1995 GeoSystems Global Corp.

Access:

Baddeck is located on the shore of Bras d'Or Lake, on Cape Breton Island. It is located on the route of the Trans Canada Highway, 67 km (40 mi.) west of North Sydney. Bus service is available.

Ferries depart from North Sydney, Nova Scotia, for Newfoundland. Airport service is also available from Sydney.

Accommodations:

Services are available at many places along this famous route; you will pass several campgrounds, hostels, motels, and bed-and-breakfast inns along the way. Campgrounds are also available in Cape Breton Highlands National Park.

Route Description:

This spectacular, challenging tour takes you through mountainous terrain. You will pass along a rugged coastline, with picturesque views of rocky coves, river gorges, sandy beaches, and majestic cliffs. There are some tough climbs on twisting roads as you tour the Cabot Trail on Nova Scotia's Cape Breton Island.

Begin your tour at Baddeck, the location of the Alexander Graham Bell National Historic Park. Take the Cabot Trail north through Middle River; Finlayson; Northeast Margaree (the Margaree River is known for its salmon fishing); Margaree Harbour, with its magnificent view of the Northumberland Strait; Cheticamp, a French Acadian village; and Petit Etang, where the Acadian Trail, a hiking trail, will take you to a panoramic view of the Cheticamp area.

The entrance to Cape Breton Highland National Park is 5 km (3 mi.) from Cheticamp. Cycle through a narrow valley and then climb Cap Rouge, where you have great views of

Cheticamp and the water below you. At French Mountain, the road climbs steeply inland. Then ride along a plateau and descend Mackenzie Mountain, via a series of switchbacks, to Pleasant Bay, 44 km (27 mi.) from Cheticamp. Near Pleasant Bay is the Lone Sheiling, a replica of the stone huts used by the first Scottish settlers to protect themselves from the winds.

Leaving Pleasant Bay, you make the toughest climb of this tour, up North Mountain, and then another sharp descent. The road hugs the cliffs along the gorge of the North Aspy River Valley. You then arrive at a scenic view of the Sunrise Valley.

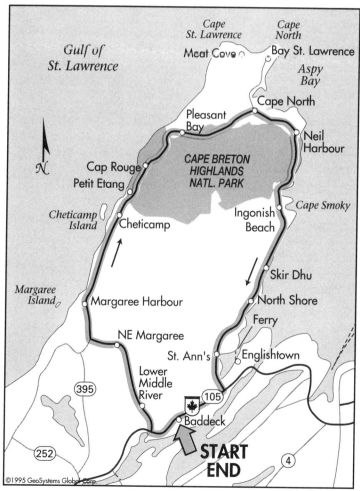

Cape North, 29 km (18 mi.) from Pleasant Bay, is the northernmost point of the Cabot Trail. From here, cycle east to South Harbour and Neil Harbour and then south to Black Brook and Ingonish. One of the oldest settled areas on the Atlantic seaboard, Ingonish offers scenic outlooks, hiking trails, parks, and beaches.

Cycle from Ingonish to Ingonish Beach, which is the exit point from Cape Breton Highlands National Park.

Cape Breton Highlands National Park is a wildlife sanctuary. The wildlife includes lynx, red fox, beaver, mink, hare, white-tailed deer, black bear, and moose. Among the 200 species of birds found in the park are red-tailed hawks and bald eagles.

Leaving the park, climb Cape Smokey, often capped by mist. You can take a ski lift to ascend from the Cape Smokey ski area for a magnificent view (on a clear day) of the Atlantic Ocean and the rugged Cape Breton coast.

Descend from Cape Smokey, and continue to cycle along the coastline. You will pass small fishing villages, including Skir Dhu (Gaelic for "black root") and North Shore. Plaster Provincial Park is near North Shore. From this park you can view Bird Islands, where many seabirds nest during the summer.

Continue to ride from North Shore to St. Ann's, site of the Gaelic College. The only school of its kind in North America, the Gaelic College preserves the Highland's heritage by offering courses in Gaelic singing, clan lore, and bagpipe playing.

Cycle on the Cabot Trail until you meet No. 105 (the Trans Canada Highway, with its wide paved shoulder); head west on No. 105 back to Baddeck, 31 km (19 mi.) from St. Ann's.

The Cabot Trail is a circle tour of the western and eastern shores of Cape Breton Island, passing through many tiny villages famous for their traditional fiddlers and folk singers. As you cycle around this northern section of Cape Breton, you view the Gulf of St. Lawrence to the west and the Atlantic Ocean to the east. Renowned inventor Alexander Graham Bell noted that "I have seen the Canadian and American Rockies, the Andes and the Alps and the

Highlands of Scotland, but for simple beauty, Cape Breton outrivals them all."

Ride to Louisburg National Historic Park:

Cycle on the Trans Canada Highway (No. 105) from Baddeck to Sydney. Then ride southeast on No. 22 to Louisburg National Historic Park (108 km/65 mi. from Baddeck). Here you will see the massive fortress erected by the French between 1720 and 1745. Costumed guides take you on a tour of the fortress.

Optional Activities:

Canoeing or fishing on the Margaree River.

At Petit Etang is the Acadian Trail, a lengthy hiking trail to the top of the Highlands for a panoramic view of the Cheticamp area (about a 4-hour hike).

The Cheticamp River offers salmon fishing. The salmon pools can reached by way of a scenic hiking trail. Licenses can be obtained at information centers.

There are several hiking trails in Cape Breton Highlands National Park, from easy strolls to challenging overnight

Cyclists on the Evangeline Trail stop to view the Minas Basin—see tour description on pages 94–97. (Photo courtesy Tourism Nova Scotia)

backpacking trips. A brochure of the trails is available from the information centers.

Deep-sea fishing is offered from several of the villages.

For more information:

For information about Louisburg National Historic Park, phone (902) 733-2280.

Superintendent
Cape Breton Highlands National Park
Ingonish, Nova Scotia B0C 1L0
Telephone (902) 285-2270

Chapter 10

Ontario

The tours in this book will prove to you that there is more to Ontario than large cities and hectic traffic; in fact, several of these cycling expeditions take you on relatively quiet country roads and bicycle paths, even in populated southern Ontario.

Ontario is a very large province, and there are many interesting cycling areas not covered on these specific trips (particularly in the north); however, these specific tours are intended to take you away on peaceful excursions while still near some of the most popular, crowded tourist regions.

Many of Ontario's roads are without paved shoulders, so use caution. These specific tours have avoided the heaviest traffic routes.

Summer temperatures in Ontario average 25°C (77°F).

In this chapter, 4 different routes are described, ranging from a 1-day recreational trip at Niagara Falls to a 4-day tour of Prince Edward County.

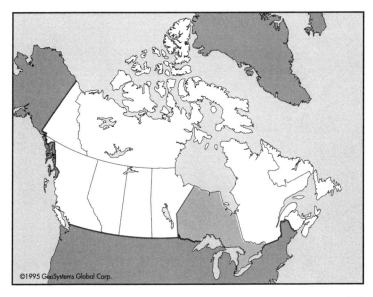

©1995 GeoSystems Global Corp.

For more information:

Canadian Hostelling
Association
209 Church St.
Toronto, Ont. M5B 1Y7
Telephone (416) 363-0697

Ontario Cycling Association,
1220 Sheppard Ave.
East Willowdale, Ont. M2K
2X1 Telephone (416) 495-4141
FAX (416) 495-4038

They publish a yearly *Guide to Cycling in Ontario*, listing clubs, tours, events, and competitions.

Ontario Travel
Queen's Park
Toronto, Ont. M7A 2E5
Telephone 1-800-668-2746
(English) or 1-800-268-3736
(French); in the Toronto area,
phone (416) 965-4008

Ontario Travel has separate guides available on accommodations, country inns, bed-and-breakfasts, camping, events, and available outdoor activities.

Manitoulin Island

Distance: 145 km (87 mi.)

Duration: 2–3 days

Rating: moderate

Type: loop route

Access:

South Baymouth can be reached by taking a 2-hour ferry ride from Tobermory, a popular tourist area on the Bruce Peninsula, or by exiting the Trans Canada Highway (No. 17) at Espanola and heading south on No. 6.

Accommodations:

There are several campgrounds, bed-and-breakfast inns, and lodges on Manitoulin Island. Full services are available at Tobermory and Espanola.

Route Description:

Several Indian reservations and quiet villages are to be found on the world's largest freshwater-surrounded island, blessed with a picturesque shoreline and numerous lakes and bays. Manitoulin Island is 150 km (90 mi.) in length and ranges from 5 km (3 mi.) to 75 km (47 mi.) in width. The island's rugged north shore has cliffs overlooking fjord-like bays; the south shore of Manitoulin Island is primarily flat plains.

This ride takes you around Lake Manitou, thought to be the world's largest lake within a lake. There is no paved shoulder for most of this route, but traffic should be relatively light. Be on the lookout for several species of birds as you cycle on Manitoulin Island, including turkey vultures, loons, cranes, ravens, hummingbirds, and hawks.

An annual Indian Pow Wow is held each August at Wikwemikong on Manitoulin Island.

Begin your loop tour at South Baymouth. Cycle along No. 6 for 13 km (8 mi.), then head northwest on No. 542 to Sandfield and Mindemoya. Turn north on No. 551 to West Bay, an Indian reserve. Turn east on No. 540, and cycle for

30 km (18 mi.) along the base of the escarpment to Little Current. The bridge at Little Current has only one lane. Watch the lights; the bridge swings open for boats.

Cycle south from Little Current on No. 6 through Sheguiandah (where there is a long climb to 10 Mile Point, a scenic outlook) and Manitowaning. The Assiginack Museum is located in what used to be the island's jail in Manitowaning. Complete your loop tour by returning to South Baymouth.

Ride North:

From Little Current, cycle north to Espanola (through the LaCloche Mountains), where you meet the Trans Canada Highway (No. 17).

Ride South on the Bruce Peninsula:

This route is described in Chapter 15. There is no paved shoulder as you cycle on the Bruce Peninsula.

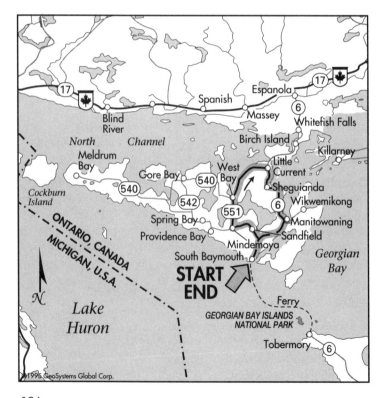

Optional Activities:

Visit Tobermory:
Take the ferry to Tobermory, at the tip of the Bruce Peninsula.
Here, you can do any of the following:
    Scuba diving in Fathom Five National Marine Park
    Take a sea cruise to Flowerpot Island, site of picturesque
        water-eroded rock formations.
    Charter a fishing boat.
    Hiking on the 725 km (435 mi.) Bruce Trail.

For more information:

For Manitoulin Island ferry information, contact:

Ontario Northland Marine Services
1155 First Ave. West
Owen Sound, Ont. N4K 4K8
Telephone 1-800-265-3163

Manitoulin Island Association
Box 119
Little Current, Ont. P0P 1K0

Niagara Falls Recreational Trail

Distance: 56 km (34 mi.)

Duration: 1 day

Rating: easy

Type: one-way tour

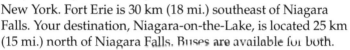

Access:

The Peace Bridge links Fort Erie, Ontario, and Buffalo, New York. Fort Erie is 30 km (18 mi.) southeast of Niagara Falls. Your destination, Niagara-on-the-Lake, is located 25 km (15 mi.) north of Niagara Falls. Buses are available for both.

Accommodations:

You will find an abundance of accommodations in this major tourist area.

Route Description:

The Niagara Falls Recreational Trail is a 56 km (34 mi.) route from Fort Erie to Niagara-on-the-Lake, amid vineyards, orchards, beautiful flower gardens, and several popular tourist sites. The route is relatively flat and includes Canada's very popular tourist attraction Niagara Falls. You share this trail with many walkers, joggers, and rollerbladers. The trip is very picturesque as you cycle along the Niagara River, past many beautiful homes; however, you cross several sideroads and driveways, so use caution. Also, the trail seems to disappear in Niagara Falls, as there are so many tourists walking; it is best to cycle on the roads through the city, still following the river; you may rejoin the actual trail near the whirlpool rapids on the Niagara Parkway.

Begin this tour at Fort Erie, a major point of entry into Canada (the Peace Bridge links Fort Erie, Ontario, with Buffalo, New York). Fort Erie was settled by United Empire Loyalists in 1748. One of Ontario's oldest race tracks, Fort Erie Race Track, is located here, as is the restored Old Fort Erie, where guards dress in early 19th-century uniforms.

Cycle on the Niagara Falls Recreational Trail from Fort Erie to Niagara Falls, where you can view the magnificent falls and enjoy the many tourist attractions.

Discovered by Father Hennepin in 1678, Niagara Falls mesmerizes millions of visitors each year with its thunderous sound and penetrating mist. The American Falls is higher and slimmer; the Canadian Falls are known as Horseshoe Falls because of the deep curve to the width of the cataract. Niagara Falls is considered to be the honeymoon capital of Canada.

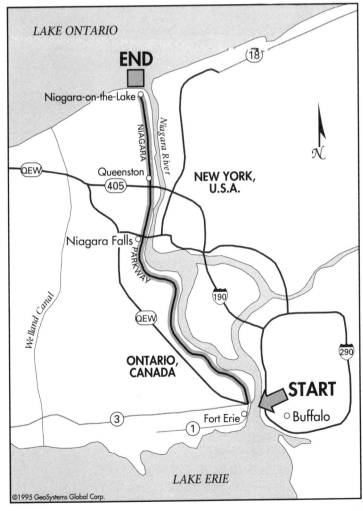

The Niagara River is one of the shorter rivers of the world, but also one of the wildest; ships from the Great Lakes use the Welland Canal to circumvent this part of the river at Niagara Falls.

Continue to follow the Niagara River as you cycle from Niagara Falls to Queenston Heights, 11 km (6.5 mi.) from the actual falls.

At Queenston Heights, you can get a panoramic view of the area by climbing the spiral staircase to the top of the Brock Monument. You can also view the Laura Secord Monument in Queenston Heights Park, the site of the Battle of Queenston Heights during the War of 1812.

Queenston Heights serves as the beginning/ending point of the Bruce Trail, a 725 km (435 mi.) hiking trail between Queenston Heights and Tobermory (at the northern tip of the Bruce Peninsula).

Continue north on the Niagara Falls Recreational Trail from Queenston Heights to Niagara-on-the-Lake, situated on Lake Ontario at the mouth of the Niagara River. Niagara-on-the-Lake is also the home of the Shaw Festival, where the plays of George Bernard Shaw are performed each summer, and the site of the Fort George National Historic Park. There are many well-preserved 19th-century homes in this picturesque little town, which served as Ontario's first capital (from 1791 to 1796). An interesting place to shop, Niagara-on-the-Lake has a number of quaint little specialty stores, and the surrounding area is a mixture of vineyards and fruit trees.

Ride to the Welland Canal:

A side trip will take you to a view of the 44 km (26 mi.) Welland Canal, which crosses the Niagara Peninsula about 13 km (8 mi.) west of Niagara Falls. This canal provides passage for cargo ships between Lakes Erie and Ontario.

Optional Activities:

There are many tourist attractions along this route, including:
    Helicopter tours
    Jet-boat rides on the Niagara gorge
    Boat ride by the falls on the Maid of the Mist
    Niagara Spanish Aerocar (cable car ride over the gorge)

Boardwalk tour along the gorge (at Great Gorge)
Walk under the falls (from Table Rock House)
Floral Clock
Niagara Falls Commission School of Horticulture
Queenston Heights
The beautiful parks and the actual falls
Marineland and Game Farm
Maple Leaf Village
Old Fort Erie
Shaw Festival
Fort George National Historic Park
Several museums, lookout towers, simulated rides,
    and other entertainments
Tours of the Niagara Falls area are available.

Take a self-guided walking tour in Niagara-on-the-Lake. For information, contact:

Chamber of Commerce
153 King St., Masonic Lodge
Niagara-on-the-Lake, Ont. L0S 1J0
Telephone (905) 468-4263.

Hike on the 725 km (435 mi.) Bruce Trail, which begins and ends at Queenston Heights.

For more information:

Niagara Falls Canada Visitor and Convention Bureau
5433 Victoria Ave.,
Niagara Falls, Ont. L2G 3L1
Telephone (905) 356-6061 or 1-800-563-2557

Prince Edward County

Distance: 220 km (132 mi.)

Duration: 3–4 days

Rating: easy

Type: loop route

Access:

Belleville is located on the Bay of Quinte, about 190 km (115 mi.) east of Toronto and 220 km (132 mi.) west of Ottawa. The major road artery for southern Ontario, No. 401, goes through Belleville, making it easily accessible. Train and bus services are available.

Accommodations:

A great variety of accommodations are available on this route, from campgrounds to motels and bed-and-breakfast inns. Camping is available in Sandbanks Provincial Park.

Route Description:

Quinte's Isle, a beautiful peninsula just south of Belleville, offers the cyclist relatively quiet roads that meander through fertile farmland and past sandy beaches; the terrain is quite flat on this loop tour. Much of this route is cycled on roads without a paved shoulder, but the relative tranquility of the area makes this an enjoyable bicycle trip.

Begin this trip at Belleville, "the friendly city," located at the mouth of the Moira River, on the beautiful Bay of Quinte. Belleville was settled by United Empire Loyalists in 1784 and incorporated in 1878. Music chimes from the clock tower of City Hall. While here, you might like to visit the Hastings County Museum, the picturesque harbor area, Corby Park (where thousands of roses bloom), Riverside Park (with its annual chrysanthemum display), and Zwicks Island Park. A Waterfront Festival is held in this city each July.

Leaving Belleville, cross the bridge on No. 62 into Prince Edward County. At Rossmore, turn west on No. 3 (the Rednersville Road) to Rednersville, past many beautiful waterfront homes on the Bay of Quinte. At Rednersville, you might decide to visit the Country Store, the oldest continuously operated general store in Ontario.

Continue west on No. 3 from Rednersville to Albury and Carrying Place, where Indians used to portage from the Bay of Quinte to Wellers Bay on Lake Ontario. Turn south on No. 33 (the Loyalist Parkway) to Consecon. The many Indian artifacts found in this area have established it as the site of the Iroquois Indian village of Kente, now anglicized into Quinte; a historical plaque refers to the Kente Mission.

From Consecon, continue on No. 33 past North Beach (which has a bay-mouth sandbar protecting it from Lake Ontario) to Wellington, where the Wellington Community Historical Museum is housed in an old Quaker Meeting House. Turn east at Wellington (still on No. 33) and ride to Bloomfield, the heart of early Quakerism in Prince Edward County.

Leave Bloomfield by cycling southwest on No. 12 for 10 km (6 mi.) to Sandbanks Provincial Park. Here, you can camp on

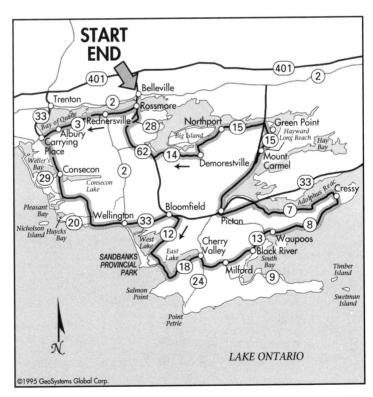

©1995 GeoSystems Global Corp.

the shore of Lake Ontario and enjoy the ocean-like setting. Beautiful sand dunes and a long, sandy beach welcome you.

After enjoying this exquisite park, cycle past East Lake and Salmon Point. Head east on No. 18 to Cherry Valley (yes, there are apple and cherry trees in this area). Turn southeast on No. 10, and ride to Milford. Cycle east on No. 17 to Black River (where fine cheddar cheese has been made since 1901), and then there is a steep climb out of Black River. Take No. 13 northeast around Smiths Bay with a scenic outlook at Rutherford Stevens Lookout. Descend into Waupoos (an Indian word meaning 'running rabbit').

Continue east along the water. Cycle around the point near Cressy. Then turn west on No. 7 and cycle along the Adolphus Reach to Glenora, where you can take a ferry across the Bay of Quinte to the mainland at Adolphustown. At Glenora, turn west on No. 44 to Lake-on-the-Mountain, a scenic outlook and a fascinating glimpse of a lake high above the Picton Bay. Rejoin No. 33 and cycle west into Picton.

Sir John A. Madonald, Canada's first Prime Minister, was raised in the quaint resort town of Picton; he began his career as a lawyer here. While in Picton, you might like to visit Macauley Heritage Park, which includes a restored church and house (now museums) and Birdhouse City (with its collection of designer birdhouses).

Take No. 49 northeast from Picton, past the Canada Cement Plant and the White Chapel (one of the earliest Methodist churches in Upper Canada) to Woodville and Roblin Mills. Turn east on No. 15, passing Mount Carmel and Green Point, where speedboat races are held at Hayward Long Reach. Cycle under the Deseronto Bridge, and ride west on No. 15 through Solmesville and Northport, to Demorestville.

Take No. 14 west and cycle past the Sunset Lookout to No. 62. Then turn north on No. 62, past the Mountain View Airport, for 8 km (5 mi.) to the Massassaga Road (No. 28). Cycle northeast on No. 28 to Rossmore, and then return to Belleville on No. 62.

Ride to Kingston and Wolfe Island:

At Glenora, take the ferry across the Bay of Quinte to Adolphustown, and then cycle on No. 33 to Kingston 52 km

(31 mi.), a city with many early Canadian landmarks. For more information, contact:

Greater Kingston Tourist Information Office
209 Ontario St.
Kingston, Ont. K7L 2Z1
Telephone (613) 548-4415

From Kingston, another ferry will take you to Wolfe Island, where there are miles of flat cycling with little traffic. If you wish, you can cycle across Wolfe Island and take a ferry to New York State (in the U.S.).

Ride to Algonquin Provincial Park:

Cycle north from Belleville (on No. 62) to Maynooth. Then ride on No. 127 and No. 60 to Algonquin Provincial Park. You ride on hilly terrain as you cross the park and cycle to Dwight 260 km (156 mi.) northwest of Belleville. Algonquin Provincial Park offers easy as well as challenging hiking and mountain biking trails, a network of canoe routes (covering more than 1,500 km (900 mi.), and many opportunities for fishing and camping. Naturalist services, interpretive programs, and conducted trips are all available. For information, phone (705) 633-5572.

Optional Activities:

Enjoy the sand dunes and swimming at Sandbanks Provincial Park.

Cycle over the Deseronto Bridge (north on No. 49) to view the Mohawk crafts on the Tyendinaga Indian Reserve.

For more information:

Quinte's Isle Tourist Assoc.
116 Main St.
Picton, Ont. K0K 2T0

Sandbanks Provincial Park
R.R. No. 1
Picton, Ont. K0K 2T0
Telephone (613) 393-3314

Thousand Islands Bikeway

Distance: 77 km (46 mi.)

Duration: 1–2 days

Rating: Easy

Type: Loop route

Access:

Gananoque is located 35 km (21 mi.) east of Kingston, in the beautiful Thousand Islands tourist area. Buses and trains are available. Gananoque is also accessible by water.

Accommodations:

There are several campgrounds and motels along this route. Camping is available on several islands in St. Lawrence Islands National Park.

Route Description:

The famous Thousand Islands Bikeway is an excellent 37 km (22 mi.) route from Gananoque to Brockville. You may be joined by walkers, rollerbladers, and joggers on this motorless paved path, but there is no worry about motor vehicles (except when you cross driveways and sideroads). Traveling east from Gananoque, the breeze is often at your back, and most of the route is slightly downhill as you travel past two provincial parks and the St. Lawrence Islands National Park.

Leaving Gananoque, ride the magnificent bike path to Ivy Lea (site of the Ivy Lea Bridge to the U.S.), Rockport, and Mallorytown Landing, headquarters of the St. Lawrence Islands National Park; campsites are available on several of the islands, and these are accessible by boat.

The paved bicycle path ends west of Brockville (where the province's oldest newspaper, the *Recorder*, has been published since 1821). Take No. 2 west from the end of the bike path back to Gananoque 40 km (24 mi.).

Gananoque is a popular resort town on the St. Lawrence River and is considered to be the gateway to the Thousand

Islands. You can take a boat tour of the beautiful Thousand Islands, stopping at Boldt Castle. You can also take a scenic flight over the islands.

Ride to Cornwall:

At the eastern end of the Bikeway, cycle east on No. 2, along the St. Lawrence Seaway. You can follow this flat route 110 km (66 mi.) to Cornwall (described in Chapter 15).

Ride to Ottawa:

At the eastern end of the Bikeway, cycle east on No. 2 to Cardinal. Cycle north on No. 22, and then follow along the banks of the Rideau Canal on No. 19 to Ottawa (130 km/78 mi.). Ottawa has over 100 km (60 mi.) of bicycle trails. The National Capital Commission will provide you with maps. An information center is located at 14 Metcalfe St.; phone (613) 239-5000 or 1-800-465-1867 (in Canada).

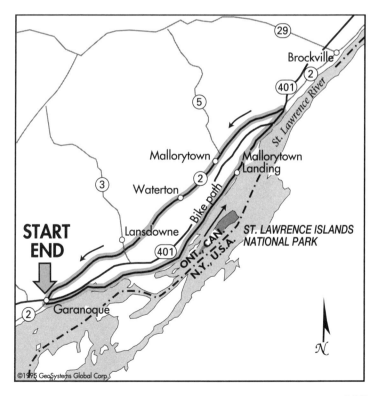

Address all written inquiries to:

The National Capital Commission
161 Laurier Ave. W.
Ottawa, Ont. K1P 6J6

Ottawa Tourist Information has a 24-hour phone service:
(613) 692-7000.

Optional Activities:

Boat or air tours of the Thousand Islands from Gananoque.

Camping on an island in St. Lawrence Islands National Park.

More information about the Ottawa area is available from:
Ottawa Tourism and Convention Authority,
111 Lisgar St.
2nd Floor
Ottawa, Ont. K2P 2L7
Telephone (613) 237-5150.

For more information:

St. Lawrence Islands National Park
Box 469, R.R.No. 3
Mallorytown, Ont. K0E 1R0

Chapter 11

Prince Edward Island

Light constant breezes and low humidity combine with an average summer temperature of 23°C (74°F) to make Prince Edward Island a very pleasant environment for the cyclist.

Prince Edward Island is served by three regional carriers (Air Atlantic, Air Nova, and Inter-Canadien) as well as Air Canada and Canadian Airlines International. Two ferry services operate between the island and the mainland. Marine Atlantic sails between Cape Tormentine, New Brunswick, and Borden, P.E.I. (14 km/8.5 mi.; a 45-minute trip); Northumberland Ferries Ltd. sails between Caribou, Nova Scotia, and Wood Islands, P.E.I. (22 km/13 mi.; a 75-minute trip). Ferry rates and schedules are available from the Tour the Island Information Centre.

The main roads are paved, but if you choose to cycle on some of the country roads, you may find red clay; these roads can pose a problem after a rain.

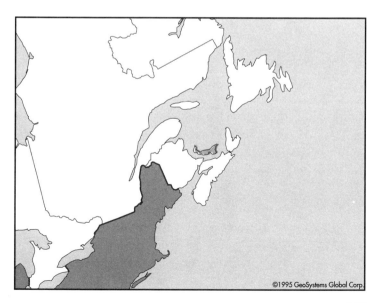

©1995 GeoSystems Global Corp.

For more information:

P.E.I. Cycling Information
Visitors Services Division
P.O. Box 940
Charlottetown, P.E.I. C1A 7M5
Telephone 1-800-463-4734

Prince Edward Island
Convention Bureau
11 Queen St.
Charlottetown, P.E.I. C1A 4A2
Telephone (902) 368-3688

Visitor Services Division
P.O. Box 940
Charlottetown, P.E.I. C1A 7M5
Telephone 1-800-561-0123

Prince Edward Island Hostel
Association
153 Mount Edward Road
Box 1718
Charlottetown, P.E.I. C1A 7N4
Telephone (902) 894-9696

Tour the Island Information
Centre
Oak Tree Place
University Ave.,
Charlottetown, P.E.I.
Telephone 1-800-565-7421 (in
the Maritimes) or
1-800-565-0267 (for the
remainder of North America)

Prince Edward Island National Park

Distance: 35 km (21 mi.)

Duration: 1–2 days

Rating: easy

Type: one-way tour

Access:

Dalvay Beach, headquarters of Prince Edward Island National Park, is located 25 km (15 mi.) north of Charlottetown. Cavendish is located at the western end of the park, 35 km (21 mi.) from Dalvay Beach.

Accommodations:

A great variety of accommodations are available in this resort area (including campgrounds within the park).

Route Description:

Cycling is very popular in Prince Edward Island National Park. There is a wide paved shoulder along the relatively flat Gulf Shore Parkway, offering a scenic tour along 40 km (24 mi.) of saltwater beaches on the Gulf of St. Lawrence, with views of sweeping sand dunes and salt marshes that abound with shore birds. Many years of erosion have carved the park's red sandstone cliffs. As you cycle through the park, there are many paths and boardwalks that lead to the water, giving you opportunities to view some of the finest beaches in eastern Canada.

Begin your tour at Dalvay Beach, headquarters of Prince Edward Island National Park, located 25 km (15 mi.) from Charlottetown. At the park's eastern edge, the dunes of Bloomington Point stretch across the mouth of Tracadie Bay.

Head west on the Gulf Shore Parkway, along the beaches and sand dunes. Stanhope Beach is a popular windsurfing area. Continue cycling past the Brackley Marsh (a stopover for migrating birds) and on to Brackley Beach. Cross the causeway to Rustico Island, home to a protected colony of great blue herons.

Leave this section of the park by heading east on No. 15 and No. 6 to North Rustico, one of Prince Edward Island's most picturesque villages. Then return to the park, continuing east past Orby Park to Cavendish, your destination. A 6 km (3.5 mi.) bike trail helps you explore the Cavendish area.

Cavendish was affectionately described in Lucy Maud Montgomery's stories *Anne of Green Gables* and *Anne of Avonlea* (among others). Lucy Maud Montgomery's Cavendish home and Green Gables House (a residence often visited by the author and thought to be a major influence for the setting of the Green Gables series) are located in this area.

Several hiking trails in Prince Edward Island National park provide further opportunity for exploration. Over 200 species of birds are found in this park, including Swainson's thrush, piping plover, northern phalarope, and slate-colored junco.

You can enjoy a traditional lobster supper in this popular region of Prince Edward Island.

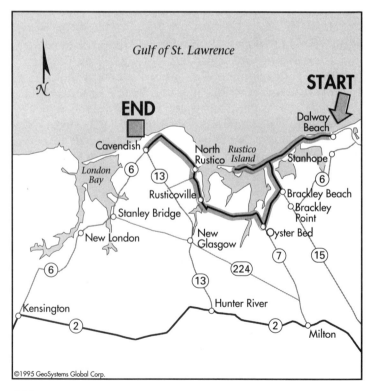

Ride to Dalvay Beach:

You can return to your starting point by retracing your steps, once again cycling past the sandy, wind-swept beaches of beautiful Prince Edward Island National Park.

Ride to Charlottetown:

From the destination of Cavendish, cycle southeast on No. 13 and then No. 2 to Charlottetown, the capital of Prince Edward Island. This 40 km (24 mi.) route is relatively flat.

Optional Activities:

Windsurfing.

Fishing charters (for tuna, cod, and mackerel) are available.

Prince Edward Island National Park offers lawn bowling, golf, and tennis. Hiking trails include:
    Bubbling Spring, Farmlands, and Reeds and Rushes
        (in the Dalvay-Stanhope area)
    Balsam Hollow and Haunted Woods
        (near Green Gables House at Cavendish)
    Homestead Trail is a combined hiking and cycling loop
        5.7 km (3.5 mi.) starting at Cavendish Campground.

For more information:

Cavendish Promotions Inc.
P.O. Box 10
Cavendish, P.E.I. C0A 1N0
Telephone :
(902) 566-1252 (winter)
(902) 963-2078 (summer)

District Superintendent,
Parks Canada , P.E.I.
P.O. Box 487
Charlottetown, P.E.I. C1A 7L1
Telephone (902) 672-2664

Around Prince Edward Island

Distance: 730 km (438 mi.)

Duration: 7–10 days

Rating: moderate

Type: loop route

Access:

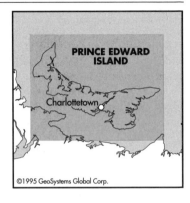

©1995 GeoSystems Global Corp.

Borden is located 56 km (33.5 mi.) southwest of Charlottetown. The ferry from Cape Tormentine, New Brunswick, docks at Borden.

Accommodations:

There are a great variety of accommodations available throughout the province; these are listed in the Visitors Guide, available through the Tour the Island Information Centre.

Route Description:

For a longer, more thorough exploration of Prince Edward Island, consider riding along the shores of what the French explorer Jacques Cartier called "the fairest land 'tis possible to see." Cycle past red-soiled farmland, fields of purple lupins, wooded lots, and protected harbors as you ride along the rather gentle coastline of Prince Edward Island, the country's smallest province (only 225 km/137 mi. long and from 6 to 66 km/4 to 40 mi. wide).

Begin your tour at the Borden ferry terminal (having arrived at P.E.I. from Cape Tormentine, New Brunswick). Take No. 1 (the Trans Canada Highway) to Carleton Siding. Then cycle west on No. 10 to Central Bedeque. Continue west on No. 1A to Reads Corner, and then turn southwest on No. 11 to Summerside.

Summerside is the principal port for potato shipments. Several older homes are found here, along with the P.E.I. Sports Hall of Fame. A summer carnival is highlighted by lobster suppers, harness racing, fiddling, and step-dancing contests.

Continue on No. 11 to Linkletter (nearby is Linkletter Provincial Park), Muddy Creek, Union Corner (another provincial park is nearby), Mont-Carmel, Cap Egmont, Maximeville, and Abram-Village.

Twin-spired churches tower by the roadside in seaside villages such as Mont-Carmel and Cap Egmont. Much of this region was settled by Acadians (French settlers from Acadia, mainland Nova Scotia); their culture is still in evidence at the Acadian Pioneer Village in Mont-Carmel (the re-creation of an early Acadian settlement), the Acadian Museum in Miscouche, and the Acadian Festival, held in Abram-Village. French is still spoken in this area.

Continue northwest along Egmont Bay, passing Baie Egmont, Higgins Road, and Enmore, and continue on No. 11 to Mount Pleasant. Take No. 2 to Inverness, Portage, and Carleton. Then turn southwest on No. 14 through Coleman, Brae, and Glenwood to West Point (near Cedar Dunes Provincial Park, with its long, sandy beach and sand dunes). The century-old wooden lighthouse, which now serves as an inn, still guides freighters and oil tankers past West Point.

Head north to Cape Wolfe; a Micmac legend surroundsitse red rocks, supposedly stained with the blood of an Indian maiden who betrayed the god Thunder. Continue cycling to Campbellton, Miminegash, Skinners Pond (where singer/songwriter Tom Connors grew up), and Seacow Pond. The North Cape is just 4 km (2.5 mi.) farther north.

The Gulf of St. Lawrence tides and the tides of Northumberland Strait meet at North Cape, P.E.I.'s windy, northernmost tip (205 km/123 mi. from Borden). An international laboratory for testing wind generators (windmills) is located at North Cape.

Along the northern shore of P.E.I., a dark, purplish seaweed called Irish moss (about half of the world's supply) is harvested by farmers and fishermen.

Cycle south on No. 12 past Anglo Provincial Park and Jacques Cartier Provincial Park (a monument commemorates his discovery of P.E.I. in 1534), Alberton, and Roxbury to No. 2; turn east on No. 2 to Portage. Then return to No. 12 through Woodbrook, Freeland, Tyne Valley (Lennox Island Micmac Reserve is nearby), Birch Hill, and Belmont (near

Winchester Cape). As you cycle to Malpeque Bay, you are in an area famous for its oysters.

Return to No. 2 at Miscouche, and ride east to Kensington. Then take No. 6 to New London (birthplace of the writer Lucy Maud Montgomery), Stanley Bridge, and Cavendish. Cycle through Prince Edward Island National Park (previously described) to Grand Tracadie and Mill Cove. Take No. 219 east to Tracadie Cross, and then ride on No. 2 northeast to Morell and St. Peters. Follow the coast of the Gulf of St. Lawrence once again by taking No. 16 to Naufrege (near Shipwreck Point), North Lake (a popular spot for tuna fishing), and East Point. The East Point Lighthouse marks the easternmost tip of P.E.I.

Cycle southwest from East Point to Souris (where you can take a ferry to the Magdalen Islands, Quebec). Take No. 2 to Dingwell Mills, No. 4 to Pooles Corner and Montague (near Buffaloland Provincial Park, where you can see herds of bison and deer), and No. 17 to Lower Montague, Murray Harbour (a busy seaport), and Murray River. Take No. 18

past Fantasyland Provincial Park (with sculptures of storybook characters) and around Cape Bear to Guernsey Cove, Northumberland Provincial Park, and Wood Islands. It's about 145 km (87 mi.) from East Point to Wood Islands.

You can take a ferry from Wood Islands to Caribou, Nova Scotia, or you can complete this loop tour of the entire island by riding on No. 1 to Charlottetown (the capital) and back to Borden.

Ride in the Magdalen Islands:

Take the ferry from Souris, P.E.I., to Cap-aux-Meules in the Magdalen Islands, Quebec (a 134 km/80.5 mi. ferry ride). This specific trip is described under the tours of Quebec.

Cycle in Nova Scotia or New Brunswick:

Take the ferry from Wood Islands to Caribou, Nova Scotia, or from Borden to Cape Tormentine, New Brunswick; both extensions are described in Chapter 15.

Optional Activities:

Visit the Acadian Pioneer Village in Mont-Carmel.

Cyclists on the Cabot Trail in Nova Scotia—see chapter 9. (Photo courtesy Tourism Nova Scotia)

Enjoy a theatrical presentation of *Anne of Green Gables* at the Confederation Centre for the Arts in Charlottetown.

Fishing (licenses are readily available at sporting outlets).

There is a wide range of water sports available (jet skiing, water skiing, swimming, windsurfing, canoeing, deep-sea fishing, ocean kayaking, etc.).

Horseback riding.

Hot air balloon rides, available near New Glasgow through Pegasus Balloons Inc., phone (902) 964-3250.

Chapter 12

Quebec

Canada's largest province, La Belle Province, contains three distinct topographical regions: the Laurentian Plateau (covering about 80% of the province and lying north of the St. Lawrence and Ottawa Rivers), the Appalachian Uplands (including the Gaspé Peninsula and the Eastern Townships), and the St. Lawrence Lowlands (the region's best farmland).

Quebec's summer temperatures are quite comfortable (averaging 24°C/75°F), and its usually mild autumn allows cycling when the kaleidoscope of blazing colors (provided by the autumn leaves) is at a peak.

For more information:

Ministry of Tourism
12 rue Ste.-Anne
Quebec City, Quebec G1R 4C4
Telephone (418) 643-2280 or
1-800-363-7777

Velo-Quebec
3575 boul. St.-Laurent,
bureau 310
Montreal, Quebec H2X 2T7
Telephone (514) 847-8356
FAX (514) 847-0242

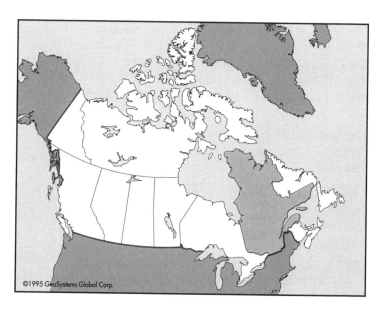

©1995 GeoSystems Global Corp.

The Gatineau Hills

Distance: 110 km (66 mi.)

Duration: 1–2 days

Rating: moderate

Type: loop route

Access:

The nation's capital, Ottawa, is located just across the Ottawa River from Hull, Quebec. Trains, buses, and air flights are available.

Accommodations:

Full services are available in both Ottawa, Ontario, and Hull, Quebec. There are camping facilities in Gatineau Park.

Route Description:

Begin this tour in Ottawa, Ontario—Canada's capital. Ottawa has over 100 km (60 mi.) of bicycle trails, and the National Capital Commission will provide you with maps of these trails.

While in Canada's capital, you might like to visit such points of interest as the Parliament Buildings, the National Gallery of Canada, the National Museum of Science and Technology, the National Aviation Museum, the National Library and Public Archives, the National Postal Museum, the National War Museum, the Royal Canadian Mounted Police Stables, and the Royal Canadian Mint. Ottawa also prides itself on its tree-lined streets and its over 70 municipal parks.

Leaving Ottawa, cross the Ottawa River into Hull, Quebec, via the Alexander Bridge, from which you can get a good view of the Parliament Buildings.

Hull, the oldest settlement in the area, is the site of the E. B. Eddy Company (a pulp and paper products factory) and a monument to St. Jean de Bréboeuf , a Jesuit missionary and martyr.

From Hull, travel on boulevard Alexander Tache (No. 148) and then north on Promenade du Lac des Fées to Gatineau

Park. Tour the park by taking the 30 km (18 mi.) Promenade de la Gatineau loop along Kingsmere Lake, Fortune Lake, and Meach Lake. Then return to Hull and Ottawa by the same route. This trip is hilly but not overly strenuous as you cycle on paved roads.

Gatineau Park is located between the Gatineau and Ottawa Rivers and encompasses 356 square km (138 square mi.) of the rocky, wooded Laurentian Mountains. An immense ice cap carved the park landscape thousands of years ago, dotting the area with about 50 lakes; the most popular recreational lakes are Lac Phillipe, Lac des Fées, and Lac la Pleche. Once the domain of Algonquin Indians, the park has about 100 varieties of wildflowers and 60 types of trees. Park wildlife includes beaver, wolf, deer, and bear; birds of the area include osprey, ruffed grouse, hawk, heron, and loon.

The scenic Gatineau Parkway (which includes a nice bicycle path) links the Lac des Fées and Lac Meach areas and

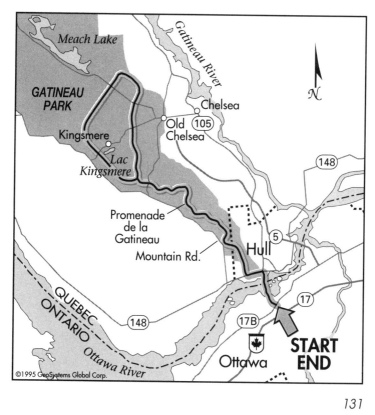

©1995 GeoSystems Global Corp.

provides access to many picnic grounds and lookouts in the unspoiled parklands.

Ride to Mont Tremblant:

This trip of 220 km (132 mi.) takes you on paved roads (with no paved shoulder much of the route) and on hilly terrain, with some tough climbs, into the scenic resort area of the Laurentian Mountains, known as Quebec's Little Switzerland.

Follow No. 17 east to Hawkesbury, and then cross into Quebec at Grenville. Follow the Ottawa River farther east (on No. 344) to St.-Andre-Est. Then ride north on No. 329 through Lachute and near St.-Sauveur-des-Monts, a beautiful village nestled in a picturesque valley (in a popular ski area). Continue on No. 329 to Ste.-Agathe-des-Monts. Then cycle west on No. 15 to St.-Jovite and northwest on No. 327 to Mont Tremblant Village, a resort on Lac Mercier. Mont Tremblant is a very popular skiing destination.

Optional Activities:

Whitewater rafting on the Ottawa River.

The Ottawa Tourism and Convention Authority has information about local sightseeing tours and self-guided walking tours. Write them at 111 Lisgar St., 2nd Floor, Ottawa, Ont. K1P 6J6, or phone (613) 237-5150.

The National Capital Commission can provide you with maps for Ottawa's bicycle trails.

Gatineau Park provides you with opportunities for camping, biking, hiking, canoeing, and fishing (license required). A brochure on mountain biking in the park is available from the Director of Gatineau Park.

For more information:

Mont Tremblant Prov. Park
Box 129
731 Chemin de la Pisciculture
St.-Faustin, Quebec J0T 2G0
Telephone (819) 688-2281

Director of Gatineau Park
161 Laurier Ave. W.
Ottawa, Ont. K1P 6J6
Telephone (819) 827-2020

Ottawa Tourist Information
24-hour telephone service:
(613) 692-7000

Horseback riders on the Magdalen Islands, Quebec—see p.139–142. (Photo courtesy Pierre Brault, Association Touristique Regionale des Iles de la Madeleine)

Laurentian Tourism
Association
14142 rue de la Chapelle
R.R. No. 1
St.-Jerome, Quebec J7Z 5T4
Telephone (514) 436-8532

National Capital Commission
161 Laurier Ave. W
Ottawa, Ont. K1P 6J6
Telephone (613) 239-5000;
1-800-465-1867 (in Canada)

The Eastern Townships

Distance: 160 km (96 mi.)

Duration: 2–3 days

Rating: moderate

Type: loop route

Access:

Sherbrooke, the largest city in
the Eastern Townships, is
located 147 km (87 mi.)
southeast of Montreal and not far from the U.S. border (close
to the states of Vermont and New Hampshire). Bus and Via
Rail service are available.

Accommodations:

Full services are available in Sherbrooke, and there are
services on the route in such places as North Hatley, Magog,
and Mont-Orford.

Route Description:

Known in French as L'Estrie, the Eastern Townships are
situated southeast of Montreal and are part of the
Appalachian Mountain chain. Quiet, hilly roads (most
without a paved shoulder), picturesque mountain scenery,
and farm-dotted countryside await you on this loop tour.

Begin your tour in Sherbrooke, the largest city in the Eastern
Townships. Once a hunting and fishing area of the Abenaki
Indians, Sherbrooke is now a center for both transportation
and industry. You can enjoy a panoramic view of the St.
Francis Valley from Beauvoir Shrine.

Cycle south from Sherbrooke on No. 143 (Queen Sud) to
Lennoxville. Then take No. 108 west to North Hatley on Lake
Massawippi. In the center of an art and culture region, North
Hatley is known for its handicrafts; several antique shops are
located here.

Continue on No. 108 to Ste.-Catherine-de-Hatley. Ride west
to Magog, a popular vacation resort, which is located on the
northern tip of Lake Memphremagog. You may enjoy

walking on the Ile-du-Marais Nature Trail, cycling on the 18 km (11 mi.) path, or taking a boat cruise on the lake.

Cycle north from Magog to Cherry River. Then ride through a section of Mont-Orford Park, a popular ski area. Mont-Orford Park offers a lodge, nature trails, boating, camping, and a nationally recognized summer music camp (with music courses, plays, films, and art exhibits).

After exploring the park, cycle southeast on No. 141, as if completing a loop back to Magog. Just before returning to Magog, exit from No. 141 and cycle south on Chemin du Bolton Est to Austin and then on to St.-Benoit-du-Lac, a Benedictine Abbey known for its chocolate, cheese, and cider.

Return the 3 km (2 mi.) to Austin, and then ride west to Bolton Centre and south on No. 245 to South Bolton. Take No. 243 northwest from South Bolton to Lac-Brome, Waterloo (famous for its mushrooms), and Warden.

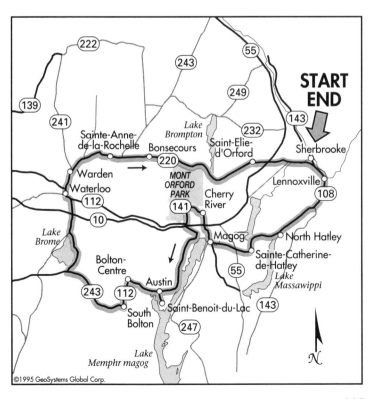

Complete this loop tour by cycling east on No. 220 through Ste.-Anne-de-la-Rochelle, Bonsecours, St.-Elie d'Orford, and back to Sherbrooke.

Ride to Montreal:

This 150 km (90 mi.) trip to the fascinating city of Montreal takes you on relatively quiet roads, although most don't have a paved shoulder. Leave the detailed tour of the Eastern Townships at Lac-Brome. Cycle west on No. 104 and south on No. 202 to Dunham. Ride southwest from Dunham (still on No. 202) to Bedford, Pike River, Noyan, and Hemmingford. Then cycle north on No. 219 and No. 221 to St.-Remi. From here, take No. 209 north and No. 132 west to Cote-Ste.-Catherine Provincial Park, one of the closest campgrounds to the city of Montreal (25 km/15 mi. from St.-Remi). The St. Lawrence Seaway Bikeway takes you from the park into downtown Montreal. There are designated bicycle routes within the city.

For a bicycle route map of Montreal, contact:

Service de la planification du territoire
2580 boulevard St.-Joseph East, 2nd Floor
Montreal, Quebec H1Y 2A2
Telephone (514) 380-6700.

A Montreal bicycling tour map (in French) can also be purchased from:
Vélo Quebec
3575 boul. St. Laurent, bureau 310
Montreal, Quebec H2X 2T7
Telephone (514) 847-8356
FAX (514) 847-0242

Bicycle Lanes of la Communaute urbaine de Montreal may be purchased from:

Canadian Cycling Association
1600 Naismith Drive, Suite 810
Gloucester, Ont. K1B 5N4
Telephone (613) 748-5629
FAX (613) 748-5692

Ride around Montreal:

A 70 km (42 mi.) ride around Montreal is recorded in the
Guinness Book of World Records as the largest cycling event in
the world. Held on the first Sunday in June each year,
participants must register, and the tour is limited to the first
45,000 cyclists. For more information, or to register, contact:

Le Tour de L'Ile de Montreal
3575 boulevard St. Laurent, bureau 310
Montreal, Quebec H2X 2Y7
Telephone (514) 847-8356
FAX (514) 847-0242.

Cycle to Quebec City:

Take No. 216 northeast from Sherbrooke to Ste.-Camille. Ride
on No. 255 to Wottonville. Rejoin No. 216, cycling to
St.-Adrien, St.-Julien, and St.-Ferdinand (on Lac William).
Then cycle on No. 265 all the way to the St. Lawrence River at
Deschaillons. From here, follow the St. Lawrence River on
No. 132 to Quebec City. As you cycle along this beautiful
river, you pass some farms that were feudal seigneuries of
colonial New France; some of these villages date from the
17th century. This relatively quiet and flat route (285
km/171 mi. long) travels primarily on paved roads without
paved shoulders, but there is a gravel section on No. 216.

You may enter Quebec City by crossing the St. Lawrence
River via the bridge, or you can continue cycling on No. 132
to Levis, where you can take a ferry to the city.

A popular cycling route in the Quebec City area is around the
Ile d'Orleans.

Informative tours are available in Montreal and Quebec City.

Optional Activities:

Visit antique shops in the North Hatley area.

Hike on the Ile-du-Marais Nature Trail or take a boat cruise
on the lake while at Magog.

Cycle l'Estiriade, a 20 km (12 mi.) paved bike path, which
links Waterloo with Granby.

For more information:

Estrie Tourism Association
25 rue de la Bocage
Sherbrooke, Quebec J1L 2J4
Telephone (819) 820-2020

The Greater Montreal
Convention and Tourism
Bureau
Mart F, 1 Frontenac
place Bonaventure
Montreal, Quebec H5A 1E6
Telephone (514) 871-1595

Mont-Orford Park
PO Box 146
Magog, Quebec J1X 3N7
Telephone (819) 843-6233

Quebec City Region Tourism
and Convention Bureau
60 rue d'Auteuil
Quebec City, Quebec
G1R 4C4
Telephone (418) 692-2471

Magdalen Islands

Distance 170 km (102 mi.)

Duration: 3–6 days

Rating: easy

Type: return trip

Access:

Souris, Prince Edward Island, is located 69 km (42 mi.) northeast of Wood Islands (the arrival point of the ferry from Caribou, Nova Scotia) and 120 km (72 mi.) northeast of Charlottetown. It is, therefore, best to combine this tour with the tours in Prince Edward Island.

The Magdalen Islands are accessible by ferry from Souris, P.E.I.; reservations are wise.

The Magdalen Islands are also accessible by air. Inter-Canadien and Air Atlantic offer daily flights; for information and reservations, phone 1-800-361-0200. Air Alliance, an Air Canada connector, offers daily flights from Gaspé, Mont-Joli, Quebec City, and Montreal; for information and reservations, phone 1-800-361-8620.

Bicycle Rental:

Bicycles can be rented and cycling information is available at Le Pedalier in Cap-aux-Meule.

Accommodations:

There are motels, inns, and designated campgrounds on the islands. For reservations, phone 1-800-363-7372.

Route Description:

The Magdalen Islands (Iles de la Madelaine) are located 250 km (150 mi.) southeast of Quebec's Gaspé Peninsula in the Gulf of St. Lawrence. Most inhabitants of these islands are fishermen who live in small port communities.

Winds may pose a problem when you are cycling on this archipelago of islands in the Gulf of St. Lawrence; however, the quiet roads, relatively flat terrain, red cliffs, stunted forests, sandy beaches, ocean views, sand dunes, fascinating caves, and quaint fishing ports make this a peaceful, picturesque destination.

Begin this trip by taking the 5-hour ferry ride from Souris, Prince Edward Island, to Cap-aux-Meules, near the midpoint of the Magdalen Islands. You can get pertinent information about the area at the Visitor Information Center. The name Cap-aux-Meules (meaning 'grindstone') comes from the presence of grindstone in the hill that overlooks the port. You can explore the area by taking a hike up Chemin de la Mine.

You can cycle on several of the Magdalen Islands by following the route suggested here (No. 199); however, specific islands can be further explored by cycling on secondary paved roads.

Take No. 199 northeast from Cap-aux-Meules to Havre-aux-Maisons, a quaint rural village; Dune du Sud, with its peat bog and fascinating caves (best explored at low

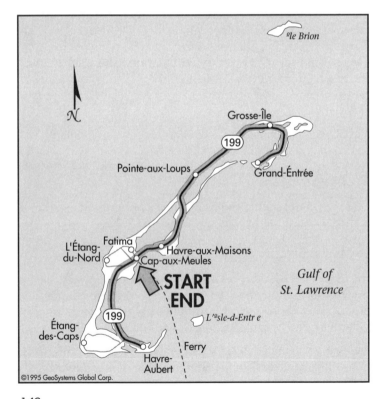

tide); Grosse Ile, with its long stretches of beautiful beaches; and Grand-Entree, known as the lobster capital of the Islands.

Return to Cap-aux-Meules, and then cycle south to Havre-Aubert, the oldest of the islands' villages. You can learn more about the culture and heritage of these islands by visiting the Musée de la Mer, where the evolution of fishing, navigation, and transportation in the gulf are illustrated. While in Havre-Aubert, visit La Grave, a popular pebbly beach (designated as a historical site).

Return the 25 km (15 mi.) to your starting point on the Magdalen Islands, and then return by ferry to Souris, P.E.I.

Ride on Prince Edward Island:

After returning by ferry from the Magdalen Islands to Prince Edward Island, cycle on this island, the smallest of Canada's provinces. Tours of Prince Edward Island have previously been described (in Chapter 11).

Ride around the Gaspé Peninsula:

This challenging, spectacular tour has been previously described (refer to the optional tours listed in Chapter 7 under New Brunswick: Bathurst to Kouchibouguac National Park). For more information, contact:

Gaspé Tourism Association
357 route de la Mer
Ste.-Flavie, Quebec G0J 2L0
Telephone (418) 775-2223

Optional Activities:

There are plentiful hiking trails/nature walks, such as:
    Chemin de la Mine, at Cap-aux-Meules
    Chemin du Basin Est and Chemin du Bassin Ouest,
        at Ile Boudreau
    The National Wildlife Reserve, at Pointe de l'Est
    Footpaths on Ile d'Entree.

Pedal-boating, canoeing, scuba diving, sailing, windsurfing.

Deep-sea fishing and diving excursion.

Gathering mollusks and seal watching at Dune du Nord, Fatima.

Glass-bottom boat tours at Havre-aux-Maisons.

Musée de la Mer at Havre-Aubert.

Horseback riding on a sandy beach on Ile du Havre-Aubert.

You can visit a large bird sanctuary, Ile Rocher-aux-Oiseaux, by boat.

For more information:

For ferry information about
the Magdalen Islands:
CTMA
P.O. Box 245
Cap-aux-Meules
Magdalen Islands
Quebec G0B 1B0
Telephone (418) 986-3278
(Cap-aux-Meules)
(902) 687-2181 (Souris)

Iles-de-la-Madelaine Tourism
Association
Box 1028
Cap-aux-Meules
Iles-de-la-Madelaine
Quebec G0B 1B0
Telephone (418) 986-2245

Chapter 13

Saskatchewan

Saskatchewan tends to have short, hot summers and long, cold winters. The average summer temperature is 24°C (75°F), but don't be surprised if you experience a temperature of 35°C (95°F) as you cycle in this prairie province. You may also at times be bothered by shifting winds.

The Trans Canada Highway (No. 1), which runs across the southern portion of the province, has a wide paved shoulder; many of the rural roads don't, but traffic is far less of a problem in these areas.

For more information:

Canadian Hostelling Assoc.,
Saskatchewan Region
628 Henderson Drive
Regina, Sask. S4N 5X3
Telephone (306) 721-2990
FAX (306) 721-2667

Saskatchewan Cycling Assoc.
2205 Victoria Ave.
Regina, Sask. S4P 0S4
Telephone (306) 780-9289

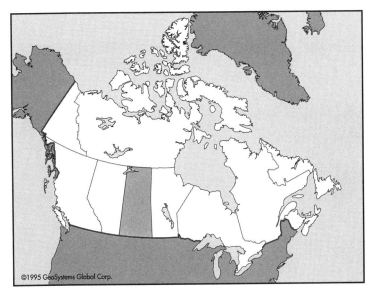

©1995 GeoSystems Global Corp.

143

Legislative building, Regina, Saskatchewan. (Photo courtesy Saskatchewan Tourism)

Tourism Saskatchewan
1919 Saskatchewan Drive
Regina, Sask. S4P 3V7
Telephone (306) 787-2300 or
1-800-667-7191
FAX (306) 787-3872

Prince Albert National Park

Distance: 184 km (114 mi.)

Duration: 2–4 days

Rating: moderate

Type: loop route

© 1995 GeoSystems Global Corp.

Access:

Prince Albert is located 141 km (85 mi.) northeast of Saskatoon, where there is an international airport. Prince Albert also has an airport. Bus service is available to Prince Albert and to the park.

Accommodations:

Full facilities are available in Prince Albert and Waskesiu. There are campgrounds in Prince Albert National Park.

Route Description:

Situated 141 km (85 mi.) north of Saskatoon, on the edge of the Precambrian Shield that extends north to the Arctic Circle, Prince Albert National Park is one of Saskatchewan's most popular destinations.

Grey Owl, the famous English naturalist who disguised himself as an Indian, made his home in this park (during the 1930s) in a little cabin (Beaver Lodge) on Ajawaan Lake. You can hike or canoe to this lake, which has been preserved by the Canadian Parks Service.

Begin your tour at Prince Albert, once the home of former Prime Minister John Diefenbaker. While here, you might like to visit the Diefenbaker House Museum, Lund's Wildlife Museum, and the Heritage Museum. Prince Albert is considered the gateway to Saskatchewan's North Country.

Cycle north on No. 2 for 77 km (47 mi.) to No. 264, then ride west for 13 km (8 mi.) to Waskesiu Lake, in Prince Albert National Park.

The park contains a 250 km (150 mi.) network of backcountry and mountain biking trails for exploring the area. The 13 km

(8 mi.) Elk Trail traverses rolling hills, but has some steep grades. Other interesting trails include the 5 km (3 mi.) Westside Boundary Road, the 44 km (27 mi.) Fifty-Seven Trail, and the 25 km (15 mi.) Narrows Tour, leading to the Narrows Campground.

After exploring Prince Albert National Park, cycle south on No. 63 (without a paved shoulder), past Emma Lake (with several beaches) and Christopher Lake. Rejoin No. 2, and head south, back to Prince Albert.

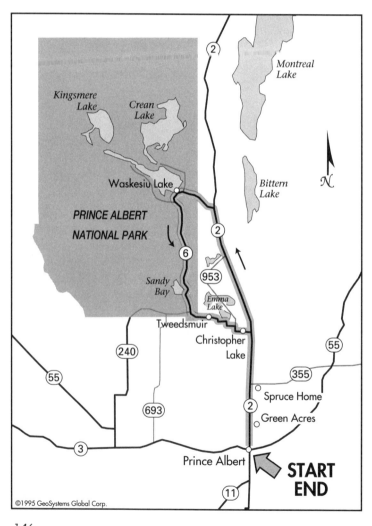

©1995 GeoSystems Global Corp.

Optional Activities:

Attractions in Prince Albert National Park include beaches, camping, biking, hiking, horseback riding, sternwheel cruises, fishing, golfing, tennis courts, and a bison compound.

Information guides for the backcountry and mountain biking trails are available from the park. Contact:
Prince Albert National Park
P.O. Box 100
Waskesiu Lake, Sask. S0J 2Y0
Telephone (306) 663-5322

Visit Grey Owl's cabin on Ajawaan Lake in Prince Albert National Park. Access is by canoeing across Kingsmere Lake or by walking on a 20 km (12 mi.) trail, with campsites en route.

Prince Albert–Batoche loop tour:

Under the leadership of Louis Riel and Gabriel Dumont, the Métis proclaimed their own government in 1885, with Batoche as capital; this was the so-called Riel Rebellion against the Canadian government. The dream of independence ended for this group when Batoche fell after a four-day siege. Riel was eventually hanged for treason (each summer, his trial is re-enacted by a theatre group in Saskatoon). You can study the history of the Riel Rebellion on this 216 km (130 mi.) loop tour.

Cycle southwest on No. 11 from Prince Albert to MacDowall. Take the gravel road to Wingard and then on to Fort Carlton Provincial Historic Park. This post was occupied by the North West Mounted Police at the time of the rebellion, and the Mounties and area settlers marched from here to do battle at Duck Lake, where they were defeated by the Métis.

Cycle east on No. 212 (still gravel) to Duck Lake, where a cairn marks the site of the Battle of Duck Lake. The Duck Lake Regional Interpretive Centre has a great number of artifacts pertaining to the Rebellion. Ride south on No. 11 (paved) to Rosthern. Then cycle east on No. 312 across the Saskatchewan River and north on No. 225 to Batoche, where the decisive battle took place, with the defeat of Louis Riel and the Métis. At Batoche National Historic Park, you can view militia trenches and a Métis cemetery, including the grave of Dumont; the history and culture of the Métis are presented in the Visitor Reception Centre.

Continue riding on No. 225 to Domremy. Then take No. 2 north to return to Prince Albert, completing this loop tour.

Ride to Saskatoon:

Cycle southwest on No. 11 from Prince Albert to Saskatoon 141 km (85 mi.), Saskatchewan's largest city. You might like to visit the Ukrainian Museum of Canada while here, with its information about the area's Ukrainian immigrants.

Just 3 km (2 mi.) north of Saskatoon is Wanuskewin Heritage Park, which preserves the life and culture of the Plains Indians. It has an on-site archaeological laboratory and dig sites. An activity area allows you to visit an Indian encampment and to try your hand at such activities as basket weaving and hide tanning.

For more information about Saskatoon, contact:

Tourism Saskatoon
Box 369
Saskatoon, Sask. S7K 3L3
Telephone (306) 242-1206

Ride to Biggar:

From Saskatoon, cycle west on No. 14 to Biggar 92 km (55 mi.), in prime grain-growing country. This is a flat ride, but you may be facing a wind.

The Qu'Appelle Valley

Distance: 105 km (63 mi.)

Duration: 1–2 days

Rating: easy/moderate

Type: loop route

Access:

Qu'Appelle is located on the Trans Canada Highway, 55 km (33 mi.) east of Regina.

Accommodations:

There are full services in Regina and camping facilities in Echo Valley Provincial Park.

Route Description:

The Qu'Appelle Valley is a marvelous, glacier-etched sunken garden stretching across much of southern Saskatchewan. The valley consists of beautiful resort villages, prime prairie farmland, and several lakes and provincial parks. Wildflowers and berries are plentiful. Several kinds of hawks soar above the peaceful valley, and ducks, geese, pelicans, and herons nest in the neighboring marshes.

According to Indian legend, a young brave who was miles from home could hear the cries of his girlfriend. He turned his canoe around and began the trip back, calling out "Qu'appelle?" (Who's calling?). Although he hurried home, when he arrived he learned that his beloved had died. It was said that from that moment on, the brave's voice could be heard echoing across the waters of the Qu'Appelle Valley.

Begin your tour of this region at Qu'Appelle, 55 km (33 mi.) east of Regina. Cycle north on No. 35 for 20 km (12 mi.) to No. 10. Then head south for 2 km (1.5 mi.) to No. 210. Ride north on No. 210, and descend into Echo Valley Provincial Park, in the heart of the scenic Qu'Appelle Valley; hiking trails, camping, fishing, boating, and swimming are all available here.

Take the B-Say-Tah Road east from Echo Valley Provincial Park to Fort Qu'Appelle, the site of a Hudson's Bay Company Trading Post built in 1864. The Fort Qu'Appelle Museum is joined to the original trading post; pioneer photos, Indian artifacts, and Hudson's Bay Company articles are displayed.

From Fort Qu'Appelle, take No. 56 south (without a paved shoulder) through Lebret and Katepwa Beach to Katepwa Point Provincial Park, on the valley floor. This small but beautiful recreational park has a great beach.

As you leave Katepwa Point Provincial Park, you face a tough climb out of the valley; you then ride through tree-dotted farmland for 16 km (10 mi.) to Indian Head. Turn west on No. 1 (the Trans Canada Highway), and cycle on the wide paved shoulder back to Qu'Appelle, your destination.

©1995 GeoSystems Global Corp.

Ride to Regina:

A 55 km (33 mi.) ride west from Qu'Appelle (on No. 1) will bring you to Regina, Canada's Queen City and the capital of Saskatchewan. Regina is the home of the Royal Canadian Mounted Police; you might like to visit the R.C.M.P. Depot and Museum. The Wascana Waterfowl Park harbors a large number of Canada geese and other waterfowl that choose to remain in Regina for the winter instead of flying south. The Devonian Pathway of Regina is an 8 km (5 mi.) paved bicycle trail that passes through six city park areas and follows the Wascana Creek.

For further information on Regina, contact:

Tourism Regina
Box 3355
Regina, Sask. S4P 3H1
Telephone (306) 789-5099

Ride to Last Mountain Provincial Historic Park:

You cycle on rolling terrain on this 48 km (29 mi.) trip. From Regina, ride northwest on No. 11 to Lumsden. Take No. 20 northeast to Craven. Tiny Craven (with a population of less than 400) hosts one of Canada's largest country music shows each July. The Big Valley Jamboree features several internationally known stars of country music. Last Mountain Provincial Historic Park is 8 km (5 mi.) north of Craven, and it preserves the site of a fur-trading outpost that operated here from 1869 to 1871; guided tours of this interesting site are available.

Ride to Moose Jaw:

A westerly ride on No. 1 of 60 km (36 mi.) takes you from Regina to Moose Jaw, home of one of the busiest airports in Canada (at the Canadian Forces Base just south of Moose Jaw) and the famous Snowbirds aerobatics team. There is a 4.5 km (3 mi.) paved walking and cycling trail at Wakamow Valley.

For further information on Moose Jaw, phone (306) 693-8097 or visit the seasonal (summer) information center on No. 1, at the site of the giant Mac the Moose.

Ride to Buffalo Pound Provincial Park:

You face a climb as you cycle north from Moose Jaw on No. 2, which has a wide paved shoulder. Ride for 19 km (12 mi.) on No. 2, and then cycle east on No. 202 for 13 km (8 mi.) to Buffalo Pound Provincial Park. Recalling the days when buffalo were herded and slaughtered in this area, the park now has a bison range, where bison can be viewed in their natural habitat. The park also features a marshland nature walk at Nicolle Flats; many species of birds reside here. Buffalo Pound Provincial Park offers camping, boating, swimming, fishing, and hiking.

For more information, contact:

Buffalo Pound Provincial Park
206 - 110 Ominica St. W.
Moose Jaw, Sask. S6H 6V2
Telephone (306) 694-3659

Optional Activities:

The Cross-Country Hang Gliding Classic is held in the Qu'Appelle Valley each September; competitors are from across Canada.

Chapter 14

The Territories

A vast, unspoiled landscape of mountains and valleys, Canada's Territories offer a special wilderness adventure for the more daring cyclist.

The Yukon Territory occupies Canada's northwesternmost corner. The Northwest Territories comprise the Arctic islands and the mainland east of the Yukon.

The roads may not be as well kept as those to the busier south; many of them are all-weather gravel. You will need to carry extra tires, and you must be prepared to be quite self-sufficient in this relatively isolated area. Take special care when being passed on the gravel roads; the stones fly and the dust is thick.

Summers are surprisingly warm way up north, with an average temperature of 15°C (59°F)—and it's daylight most of the time.

This chapter includes descriptions of 3 different tours.

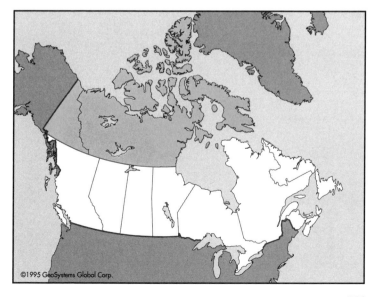

©1995 GeoSystems Global Corp.

For more information:

Hostelling International
B. C. Region
No. 402 - 134 Abbott St.
Vancouver, B.C. V6B 2K4
Telephone (604) 684-7101
FAX (604) 684-7181
(licensed hostels in B.C. and
the Yukon)

Northwest Territories Tourism
Box 1320
Yellowknife, NWT X1A 2L9
Telephone (403) 873-7200 or
1-800-661-0788.

Tourism Yukon
Government of Yukon
P.O. Box 2703
Whitehorse, Yukon Territory,
Y1A 2C6
Telephone (403) 667-5340.

Yukon/Northwest Territories
Cycling Association
c/o Gary Wilson
Box 6158
Whitehorse, Yukon Y1A 4Z2
Telephone (403) 668-4019
FAX (403) 667-2136

Whitehorse Loop

Distance: 762 km (457 mi.)

Duration: 7–10 days

Rating: strenuous

Type: loop route

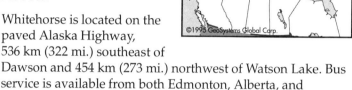

Access:

Whitehorse is located on the
paved Alaska Highway,
536 km (322 mi.) southeast of
Dawson and 454 km (273 mi.) northwest of Watson Lake. Bus
service is available from both Edmonton, Alberta, and
Vancouver, British Columbia. Contact:

Greyhound Lines of Canada
2191 - 2nd Ave.
Whitehorse, Yukon Y1A 3T8
Telephone (403) 667-2223
FAX (403) 667-2772

Daily flights are available to Whitehorse. Contact:

Canadian Airlines International Head Office
Scotia Centre, Suite 2800
700 - 2nd St. SW
Calgary, Alberta T2P 2W2
Telephone (403) 294-2000
FAX (403) 294-2066

Accommodations:

Whitehorse is the capital of the Yukon Territory and has
several types of accommodations.

This specific tour is most suitable for camping, but there are
some services available at Carmacks, Faro, Ross River,
Johnsons Crossing, and Jakes Corner.

Bike Rental:

You can rent a bicycle at Whitehorse if you prefer not to bring
one with you.

Route Description:

Whitehorse, the capital of the Yukon Territory, was founded during the Klondike Gold Rush. Its history is remembered in the poetry of Robert Service (*The Cremation of Sam McGee* is one of the poems by the Bard of the Yukon); the prose of Jack London, author of *White Fang* and *Call of the Wild*; the S.S. Klondike, one of the last sternwheelers on the Yukon River; *Frantic Follies*, a variety show; and the W. D. MacBride Centennial Museum. Annual events in Whitehorse include the Frostbite Festival, the Yukon Quest dogsled races, the Yukon Championship Dog Races, the Sourdough Rendezvous, and the Midnight Sun Golf Tournament.

Cycle north from Whitehorse on the Old Dawson Trail (No. 2) to Braeburn and Carmacks (named after one of the first men to hit the jackpot on the Klondike). Turn east on No. 4 (the Campbell Highway), which is a gravel road, and ride to Faro, which is the site of a large lead-zinc mine. Take note that when the mine is operating, this route is traveled by large ore trucks, causing dust and gravel problems. Continue

riding east on No. 4 to Ross River. Then cycle south on No. 6 (another gravel road) to Johnsons Crossing. Here you will find the paved Alaska Highway (No. 1), which you will take to Jakes Corner and then back to Whitehorse.

You are surrounded by mountains for much of this tour as you cycle by alpine meadows and forests. Be prepared, as services are limited in this area. You face some tough climbs as you cycle through the Pelly Mountains. Be on the lookout for wildlife and fresh berries.

Mountain biking on the Canol Heritage Trail:

At the junction of No. 4 and No. 6, cycle northeast, passing through Ross River (where you will find the only services on the route). This challenging wilderness journey may include fording some streams where you encounter washed-out bridges.

Spectacular Alaska-Yukon loop:

This picturesque, very challenging trip of almost 600 km (360 mi.) has you cycling in mountainous terrain in both the United States and Canada. There are several tough climbs on this route, including two mountain passes. The Canadian portion of the route is paved, but there are gravel roads after crossing the border.

Cycle west from Whitehorse on the Alaska Highway. At Haines Junction, turn south on No. 3. Cross the border and ascend the Chilkoot Pass before arriving at Haines, Alaska, in a magnificent setting. Take a ferry to Skagway, Alaska, another enchanting coastal destination. Then tackle the very strenuous climb through the White Pass (on No. 2) before returning to Canada. After crossing the border, ride to Carcross and then back to Whitehorse.

Whitehorse–Jakes Corner–Carcross loop:

This shorter loop tour is 236 km (142 mi.) in length. Cycle east on the Alaska Highway from Whitehorse to Jakes Corner. Take No. 8, a gravel road, from Jakes Corner to Carcross, a picturesque little village that was a major depot for the railway during the Gold Rush era. Then return to pavement as you cycle north on No. 2 and No. 1 back to Whitehorse.

Ride to Atlin, British Columbia:

Cycle south on No. 7 (a gravel road) from Jakes Corner, Yukon, to Atlin, British Columbia. The exquisite setting of Atlin, called the Switzerland of the North, makes this 100 km (60 mi.) trip very worthwhile. You view snow-capped mountains beyond this picturesque little town located on the edge of clear, blue Atlin Lake.

Ride the Klondike Highway:

Cycle to Dawson, in the heart of the Klondike, by riding north on No. 2 from Whitehorse. This paved road follows the famous route of the Gold Rush prospectors. This trip takes you through a vast wilderness area, but there are some services at Carmacks, Minto, Pelly Crossing, and Stewart Crossing as you cycle from Whitehorse to Dawson 536 km (322 mi.).

Optional Activities:

Fishing (license needed); many charter air services, outfitters, and guided sport-fishing trips available.

"Flightseeing" over Kluane National Park and to view Mount Logan, the highest peak in Canada.

Visit Miles Canyon:
Near Whitehorse, there is a 1 km (.5 mi.) side road to scenic Miles Canyon, with a suspension bridge.

Cruise to British Columbia:
Skagway is the northern terminus of the Alaska Marine Highway. You can take a ferry from Skagway, Alaska, and cruise the Inside Passage. You may make several stops at Alaskan ports, including Juneau, the capital of Alaska. Continue cruising down the coast until you arrive back at Canada's mainland in British Columbia.

For more information:

Whitehorse Chamber of Commerce
Whitehorse Information Centre
No. 101 - 302 Steele St.
Whitehorse, Yukon Y1A 2C5
Telephone (403) 667-7545
FAX (403) 667-4507

The Dempster Highway

Distance: 766 km (460 mi.)

Duration: 7–10 days

Rating: strenuous

Type: one-way tour

Access:

Dawson City is located in the heart of the Klondike, 536 km (322 mi.) northwest of Whitehorse (on the Klondike Highway). Bus service is available to Dawson City and from Inuvik (but not daily).

Charter flight service is available from both Dawson City and Inuvik. There are also daily flights on major airlines from Inuvik.

Accommodations:

There are relatively few services along this route; it's most appropriate for camping. There are full services in Dawson City and some services in Eagle Plains and Inuvik.

Route Description:

The only Canadian highway to cross the Arctic Circle, the Dempster Highway is a long, strenuous ride on a dirt/gravel road and rough terrain from Dawson City in the Yukon Territory, to Inuvik in the Northwest Territories. Be prepared for tire, dust, and insect problems. Heat may also be a problem, as there is almost no shade or darkness in this Land of the Midnight Sun. Furthermore, services are very limited on this route. However, most of the dirt/gravel road is in good shape, and the wilderness area that you are cycling through provides you with opportunities for viewing wildlife and spectacular scenery. Your solitude may be broken by the screech of an owl or the bark of a fox; you may even see a bear ahead of you on the road.

Begin this wilderness adventure in Dawson City, which was the center of excitement during the Gold Rush era. At that time, Dawson City was the largest city north of San Francisco and west of Winnipeg, but today there are only about 2,000 year-round residents. Many historic buildings are still to be found in Dawson City, including Diamond Tooth Gertie's, Eldorado, and The Midnight Sun.

South of town, on Bonanza Creek Road, is the Discovery Claim, which started the great stampede of prospectors. The first strike, by George Cormack and his group, was 17 August 1896. There are still opportunities to pan for gold in this area.

Southeast of town is Midnight Dome, from which you can get a magnificent view of the area. It's a tradition to visit Midnight Dome at midnight on June 21st, the longest day of

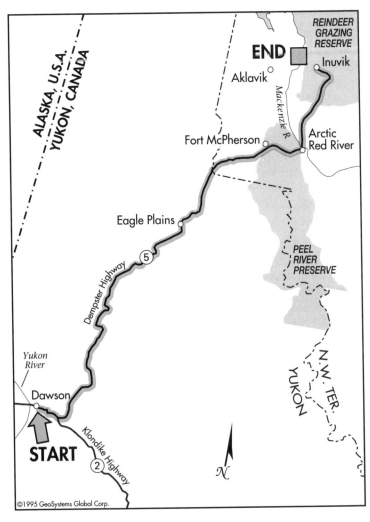

the year; it's still light enough at midnight on that day for a view from the summit.

Leaving Dawson City, cycle east on No. 2 (a paved road) to the Dempster Highway. You then begin this adventurous route on the dirt/gravel roadway as you cycle through the Ogilvie Mountains to Eagle Plains, 412 km (247 mi.) from Dawson City. You will cross the imaginary line of the Arctic Circle and cross the Richardson Mountains to get to the border of the Northwest Territories, 507 km (305 mi.) from Dawson City. You pass the Indian villages of Fort McPherson and Arctic Red River on your way to your destination of Inuvik. You make two ferry crossings on this route for the Peel and Mackenzie Rivers (these ferry crossings are replaced by ice bridges in the winter).

Your destination of Inuvik is one of the northernmost points on the North American continent that can be reached by public road. Inuvik is located on the Mackenzie delta and in a Reindeer Grazing Reserve region; it serves as a starting point for plane trips to the Arctic Ocean. Inuvik was constructed in 1954 to replace Aklavik, which seemed to be disappearing into the Mackenzie delta.

The land above the Arctic Circle overlies permafrost, a permanently frozen layer of earth that is covered by a varying amount of soil. Special construction methods are needed here; for example, houses sit atop poles driven deep into the permafrost.

There are 24 hours of daylight through much of June and July in Inuvik, so you have lots of opportunity to marvel at the wonders of this unique area at the end of your adventurous trip on the Dempster Highway.

Ride a wilderness loop:

Fly from Inuvik to Fort Simpson, and then continue your cycling adventure by riding on the Liard Highway (No. 7), which is another remote, gravel road with very few services. Ride into northern British Columbia and eventually cycle northwest on No. 97 (paved) to Toad River, Liard River, and Lower Post. Cross the border back into the Yukon Territory and ride to Watson Lake. Continue on the paved Alaska Highway (No. 1) to Upper Liard, Johnsons Crossing, Jakes

Corner, and Whitehorse. Then ride the Klondike Highway (No. 2) back to Dawson City.

Optional Activities:

See the magnificent view of Dawson City and area from Midnight Dome.

Play golf at the Top of the World Golf Course at Dawson City.

While in Dawson City, visit Diamond Tooth Gertie's Gambling Hall and enjoy entertainment reminiscent of the Klondike Gold Rush era.

Goldpanning in Bonanza Creek, near Dawson City.

Cruising on the Yukon River.

Take a flightseeing or fishing trip to Nahanni National Park, a World Heritage Site.

Wood Buffalo National Park

Distance: 300 km (180 mi.)

Duration: 3–4 days

Rating: moderate

Type: one-way tour

Access:

Hay River is situated on the south shore of Great Slave Lake and is about 1,000 km (600 mi.) northwest of Edmonton, Alberta.

You can reach Hay River by taking No. 2 and No. 35 through northern Alberta to the border and then taking No. 1 and No. 2 north in the Northwest Territories. You can also reach Hay River via the Mackenzie Highway (No. 1) from the west.

This area is highly dependent on air travel. Flights are available to Hay River and from Fort Smith.

Bus service is also available (but not daily) from Edmonton, Alberta, to Hay River, and from Fort Smith back to Edmonton.

Accommodations:

Services are available in Hay River and Fort Smith, but plan to be self-sufficient on this route. Camping is available in Wood Buffalo National Park.

Route Description:

Situated partly in the Northwest Territories and partly in Alberta, Wood Buffalo National Park is one of the largest parks in the world. Established to protect the world's largest free-roaming herd of wood bison, the vast subarctic wilderness of this park is also one of the last nesting grounds for the endangered whooping crane. Other wildlife in the park include plains bison, moose, caribou, and black bear; other birds found in the park include hawks, eagles, and pelicans.

Begin this trip in Hay River in the Northwest Territories. Situated on Great Slave Lake, Hay River serves as the headquarters of the Great Slave Lake commercial fishing industry. It's believed that the Slavey Dene Indians have used this area for thousands of years.

Leaving Hay River, cycle south on No. 2 to No. 5, then head east to the entrance to Wood Buffalo National Park. The road in the park is gravel, so be prepared for tire and dust problems. Services are very limited.

Cycle on No. 5 through a section of the park to Fort Smith. The traffic is light as you ride along this dusty road and enjoy the magnificence of this wilderness area. Wildflowers and berries are plentiful. Wood Buffalo National Park offers opportunities for camping, canoeing, and hiking.

The Northern Life Museum, in Fort Smith, examines the history of this area.

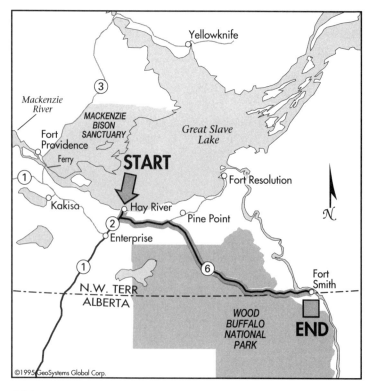

Ride to Fort Resolution:

Instead of turning south to cycle into the park, continue riding northeast on No. 6 to Pine Point. You will then cycle on a gravel road around Resolution Bay to Fort Resolution 94 km (57 mi.) from the turnoff to the park). Fort Resolution is on the southeast shore of Great Slave Lake.

Ride to Yellowknife:

Cycle, again primarily on gravel roads, from Hay River to Yellowknife, the seat of government of the Northwest Territories. Cycle southwest on No. 2, northwest on No. 1, and north on No. 3 (crossing the Mackenzie River by free ferry) on this 450 km (270 mi.) trip.

Ride on the Ingraham Trail:

You can cycle on the scenic 71 km (44 mi.) Ingraham Trail (No. 4) from Yellowknife to Tibbitt Lake (partly paved and partly gravel). Campgrounds and boat launches are found along this route. Several hiking trails lead off of the Ingraham Trail; for example, two beautiful waterfalls on the Cameron River are accessible by trails. An Ingraham Trail Map and Campground Chart is available in Yellowknife.

Ride to Edmonton, Alberta:

For an extended trip of about 1,000 km (600 mi.), cycle south from Hay River to Edmonton. You ride on paved roads with little traffic as you take No. 2 and then No. 1 (in the Northwest Territories) and No. 35, No. 2, No. 43, and No. 16 (the Yellowhead Highway) in Alberta.

Another adventurous route to Edmonton is to fly from Fort Smith (the destination of the detailed tour) to Fort McMurray, in northern Alberta. Then continue cycling by traveling southwest on No. 63 and No. 28 to Edmonton, a distance of 450 km (270 mi.) from Fort McMurray.

Optional Activities:

Fishing from Great Slave Lake.

Flightseeing over Wood Buffalo National Park.

Hiking, cycling, canoeing, and camping in the park.

For more information:

City of Yellowknife
Box 580
Yellowknife, NWT X1A 2N4
Telephone (403) 920-5600

For ferry information (for
South Mackenzie River),
phone (403) 873-7799 (in
Yellowknife) or
1-800-661-0751

For road conditions, phone
1-800-661-0750

Fort Smith Tourist
Information Bureau
56 Portage Ave.
Conibeau Park
Fort Smith, NWT
Telephone (403) 872-2515

Park Superintendent
Wood Buffalo National Park
Box 750
Fort Smith, NWT X0E 0P0
Telephone (403) 872-2237

Town of Hay River
Postal Bay 5000 (EG)
Hay River, NWT X0E 0R0
Telephone (403) 874-6522
FAX (403) 874-3237

Chapter 15

Canada Coast to Coast

This route description is detailed for the convenience of the avid cyclist who wishes to ride from coast to coast—or wants to ride across a particular province or section of the country. The route has, therefore, been divided into sections corresponding to the provinces.

Although the route can of course be traversed in either direction, it is usually recommended to ride from west to east to take advantage of the prevailing westerly winds.

The suggested route, which is the one I followed, jogs in and out of the U.S. for considerable distances. If you want to remain in Canada all the way, you can follow the alternate routes described near the end of the chapter.

I recommend the proposed route in preference to the alternates because it is by and large easier and more scenic. For instance, the recommended route follows the south shore

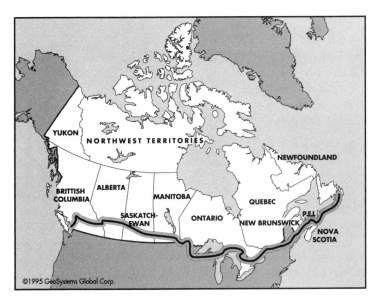

of Lake Superior (in the U.S.) because it is a flatter route, with better roads and less traffic.

On the other hand, you want to take an easier (but less scenic) route in the east, while I took the more challenging route through the eastern United States simply to ride through the picturesque, mountainous terrain of Vermont, New Hampshire, and Maine.

British Columbia

875 km (525 mi.)

Begin your trip in Vancouver, British Columbia, on Canada's west coast. Points of interest in the Vancouver area include the largest Chinatown in North America, B.C. Place, Exhibition Park, Gastown, Granville Square, Bloedal Conservatory, Capilano Suspension Bridge, Queen Elizabeth Park, Stanley Park, and the unique sunbathing area called Wreck Beach (where clothes are optional).

Much of the Trans Canada Highway is off-limits to cyclists between Vancouver and Chilliwack, so take the North Shore Route instead. Follow East Hastings St., which becomes the Barnet Highway and then the Lougheed Highway (No. 7) at Port Coquitlam. Although very busy in places, this route is relatively flat and, for the most part, has a paved shoulder all the way to Hope (site of the filming of *Rambo*).

At Hope, head north on the Trans Canada Highway (No. 1). You enter the Fraser Canyon and cycle through several tunnels cut through the rock. Be very careful in these tunnels, as the paved shoulder disappears, and the tunnels are dark. Turn on your bicycle light, remove your sunglasses, wait until no traffic is coming, and ride through the tunnels with speed.

Near Boston Bar you come to Hell's Gate, a worthwhile place to visit. When railroad builders drove their line through here in 1914, they caused a slide that almost destroyed the salmon run; the Hell's Gate Fishways were built between 1944 and 1946, and about 2 million sockeye salmon now swim up the river each year to reach their spawning grounds. About 34 million gallons of water flow through the gorge every minute (more than flows over Niagara Falls). Take the tram down into the canyon for a closer view of Hell's Gate.

You face a tough climb out of Hope and another just before reaching Hell's Gate. As you cycle through the Fraser Canyon, along the Fraser River, you will see many scenic splendors and pass rock slide areas, where cement walls have been built to prevent the rocks from sliding out onto the road.

At Lytton, the rafting capital of Canada, the Fraser and Thomson rivers join. Follow the Thomson River north (on the Gold Rush Trail) to Spences Bridge and Cache Creek.

Cache Creek is sometimes referred to as the Arizona of Canada (cactus, tumbleweed, sagebrush), and there are several ranches in this area—cattle, horses, buffalo.

Cycle east on No. 1 from Cache Creek to Kamloops. There is a 3 km (2 mi.) climb out of Cache Creek and Six Mile Hill later on. You can avoid most of the heavy traffic through Kamloops by following the designated bicycle trail. The trail takes you back out to the highway on the east side of Kamloops at Valleyview.

Ride through the rather level valley for about 50 km (30 mi.) east of Kamloops and. The riding remains quite level all the way to Salmon Arm. There's a long climb out of Salmon Arm, and then the terrain becomes hilly again. There's a long descent into Sicamous.

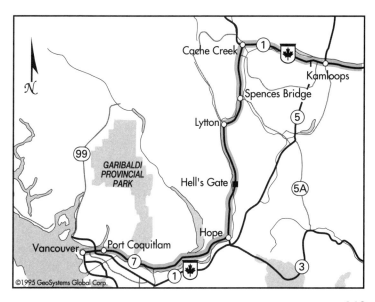

Sicamous claims to be the houseboat capital of Canada. There are over 300 commercial houseboats on Shuswap and Mara Lakes. There is a floating store at Cinnemousin Narrows so that boaters don't even have to come off the water for supplies.

From Sicamous, it's a relatively level ride to Craigellachie. Stop here at the site of the Canadian Pacific Railway's monument to the last spike, which completed Canada's rail line on November 7, 1885.

The white-capped Columbia Mountains are easily visible as you cycle from Craigellachie to Revelstoke. The Columbia Mountains are made up of the Caribou, Monashee, Selkirk, and Purcell ranges (the more famous Rocky Mountains are actually farther east, in the Lake Louise–Banff area)

At Revelstoke, you can take a helicopter tour of the area, including the Columbia Mountains, Mount Revelstoke National Park, and Glacier National Park. The Revelstoke area receives a large amount of snow annually. Near Revelstoke is the Revelstoke Dam, Canada's highest concrete dam.

There is a descent into Revelstoke and a long climb out. Then cycle on a wide paved shoulder through the park, where you may see such wildlife as deer, mountain sheep, elk, and bear. The ride is relatively easy through Mount Revelstoke National Park to Albert Canyon, with a campground and hot springs. But then there are tough climbs from Albert Canyon to the top of the Rogers Pass in Glacier National Park. Stop to enjoy the view from the top of the famous Rogers Pass. You will find a touristy, rather expensive restaurant at the summit; be prepared to stop here if it rains, as you will need dry brakes for the long, sharp descent (I had to wait here for an hour during a sudden shower). Be prepared for a dramatic change in the temperature as you reach the summit, and dress warmly for the rapid descent.

The trip from Revelstoke to the summit of the Rogers Pass is about 70 km (42 mi.), and it is about 85 km (50 mi.) from Rogers Pass to Golden. The Rogers Pass descent is long and steep, and you will ride through several avalanche sheds and the Connaugh Tunnel—be careful.

If you plan to cycle from Revelstoke to Golden in one day, remember that it is over 150 km (90 mi.). Be prepared for slow progress, at times, as there are some steep sections; however, the excellent condition of the road and the spectacular beauty of the area more than make up for the tough climbs.

The shorter ride (about 85 km/50 mi.) from Golden, British Columbia, to Lake Louise, Alberta, is even tougher. There are some narrow, treacherous sections and several steep climbs—the toughest of which is the climb out of Field and through the Kicking Horse Pass, straddling the Continental Divide in Yoho National Park. Stop to view the Spiral Train Tunnel, near the summit of Kicking Horse Pass, which will add to your awe of the area and of the incredible engineering involved in crossing the Kicking Horse Pass by train.

About 5 km (3 mi.) east of Field is a turnoff for a side trip to Takakkaw Falls, one of the highest waterfalls in North America. However, this road is steep, narrow and without paved shoulder, and the round trip would add about 30 km (18 mi.) to your journey. If you do decide to take this side trip, there is a campground and a vast network of hiking trails.

Although this makes for a couple of tough days of cycling in a row (through the Rogers Pass and the Kicking Horse Pass),

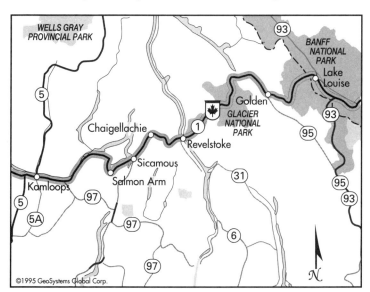

you can take pride in the fact that you have now made it through the mountains. You then cross the border into the province of Alberta and descend into Lake Louise on No. 1A.

Alberta

575 km (345 mi.)

Lake Louise is in the heart of the Rocky Mountains tourist area, so be prepared to pay more for food, accommodations, etc. Lake Louise is, indeed, very picturesque and well worth visiting. Both Lake Louise and the nearby Lake Moraine are beautiful to photograph. Lake Louise claims to be the largest ski area in Canada, with its skiable terrain spread out over 4 distinct mountain faces.

The section of the Trans Canada Highway (No. 1) from Lake Louise to Banff (about 85 km/50 mi.) is part of the Icefields Parkway (one of the most famous bicycle routes in the world—and described in Chapter 4. Because of its wide paved shoulder, I recommend this route for your ride through Banff National Park. However, No. 1A (the Bow Valley Parkway) may be slightly more scenic, with its many twists and turns and its proximity to the Bow River and Johnston Canyon and Falls; it also has less traffic but no paved shoulder.

Regardless of which route you choose, enjoy the spectacular scenery as you cycle from Lake Louise to Banff—and be on the lookout for wildlife. Fences have been built along the road to protect animals from wandering out, as several have been killed by vehicles. As I have cycled along this section, I have seen several species of wildlife, including mountain goats, deer, a herd of elk, and moose swimming across a lake.

Banff is another picturesque town in this tourist region that is well worth visiting. There are many campgrounds, restaurants, and trails for biking and hiking in this area, and many opportunities for such activities as canoeing, fishing, heli-hiking, and heli-biking. Hot springs and several other attractions are located in Banff; there is even a buffalo paddock just off No. 1.

A divided highway takes you from Banff to Canmore; the ride is quite easy, and you may even be assisted by a prevailing west wind. Canmore, site of the 1988 Winter

Olympic Games, has over 50 km (30 mi.) of trails for skiing and mountain biking.

Leave No. 1 at Canmore. Cycle on No. 1A (on the Old Bow Trail or Banff Coach Road) to Cochrane. You are now in what is called Big Hill Country; so there are still some tough climbs, even though you have left the mountains behind. From Cochrane, take No. 22 north and No. 567 east to Beseker. Continue east on No. 9 to Drumheller. This route has much less traffic than No. 1 and it avoids cycling through Calgary.

If, however, you want to visit Calgary (site of the Calgary Zoo, Botanical Garden and Prehistoric Park, Canada Olympic Park, Alberta Science Centre, the National Museum of Alberta, and the Calgary Stampede) continue from Canmore on No. 1, the busy Trans Canada Highway. Calgary has an excellent network of cycling routes. When you have finished exploring Calgary, head northeast on No. 9, joining my route near Beiseker and then continue on to Drumheller.

As you leave the mountains behind, you make a gradual transition from spruce forests to open prairie; from the foothills to a flatter, more open landscape.

Drumheller is a fascinating area to visit because of its history of being home to dinosaurs. Cycle through rich farmland, with lush fields of wheat and wide open spaces as you

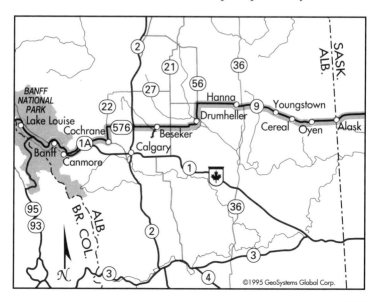

©1995 GeoSystems Global Corp.

approach the Drumheller area. Then you suddenly arrive at the badlands of the Red River Valley, which are the product of glacial activity. Stop at Horseshoe Canyon Park to view the badlands and the gophers that will pose for you and eat out of your hand; then descend into Drumheller, with fossil shops, Reptile World, and Drumheller Prehistoric Park. The Royal Tyrell Museum of Paleontology displays dinosaurs (this museum is on Dinosaur Trail). Strangely sculpted rock towers (hoodoos) are also found near Drumheller. Because of its location in a deep valley, Drumheller can be very hot during the summer. Drumheller was named after Sam Drumheller, who began the area's first coal mine operation in 1911.

A long climb is required to cycle out of Drumheller. The land again improves into rich farmland as you head east on No. 9, which has a paved shoulder and much less traffic than the Trans Canada Highway. You cycle through central Alberta, home to many ducks, hawks, foxes, and deer. The area, known as Big Country, is quite open. You will cycle through the small towns of Hanna (known as the home of the Canada grey goose), Youngstown, Cereal, Oyen, and Sibbald. The riding is quite easy, but there are still some hills, particularly between Cereal and Oyen. There is more variety to the terrain than you would find if you remained cycling on the Trans Canada Highway through Alberta.

Saskatchewan

640 km (385 mi.)

Cross the Alberta border and arrive at Alsask, Saskatchewan on No. 7, and continue east to Kindersley. This town is baseball crazy; Kindersley's ballpark holds more people than the entire population of the town. Many provincial baseball tournaments are held here; even the World Youth Baseball Tournament has been held in this small town. Kindersley also attracts many hunters in the autumn for its ducks, geese, pheasants, and partridge.

The shoulder is very rough for about 35 km (20 mi.) as you leave Kindersley. Continue on No. 7 to Rosetown about 90 km (54 mi.) Head south on No. 4 and then east on No. 15 to Outlook, site of the Saskatchewan Irrigation Development Center. As you arrive at Outlook, you cross a narrow bridge without a shoulder for cyclists, over the South Saskatchewan River, and climb a steep hill. Near the town of Outlook is Boot Hill, named after a line of boots on a fence.

There are few services for the next 170 km (106 mi.), so plan with care. You will pass Kenaston (known as the blizzard capital of Canada), Raymore, Ituna, and Melville as you cycle on No. 15 across this prairie province.

Melville was named after Charles Melville Hays, a former president of the Grand Trunk Railroad; he died on the maiden voyage of the *Titanic*.

No. 15 ends shortly after leaving Melville. Then take the Yellowhead Highway (No. 16) to Churchbridge, Langenburg, site of the World Championship Throne Races, where toilets and outhouses are raced each year, and across the border into Manitoba. The paved shoulder ends at the border.

Manitoba

567 km (340 mi.)

There is a steep climb out of the Assiniboine Valley before you reach Russell. A statue of a bull welcomes you to Russell, home of the Beef and Barley Days Festival. Continue on No. 16 from Russell to Shoal Lake, Minnedosa (hilly area), Neepawa (the birthplace of Canadian writer Margaret

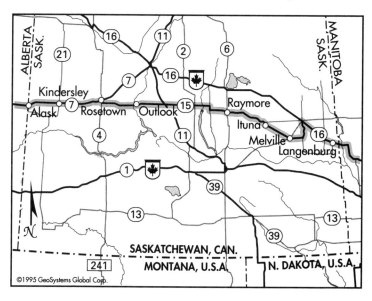

©1995 GeoSystems Global Corp.

Laurence), and Gladstone. As you cycle southeast, the terrain becomes flatter.

The Yellowhead Highway (No. 16) joins up with the Trans Canada Highway (No. 1) about 10 km (6 mi.) west of Portage la Prairie, and the paved shoulder ends. In fact, there is no paved shoulder for most of the remainder of the trip through Manitoba.

Portage la Prairie used to be considered a resting place, or portage, between the Assiniboine River and Lake Manitoba. Nearby is the Portage Spillway, to control flooding of the Assiniboine River. The Fort la Reine Museum and Pioneer Village depict life in the area in the 1800s.

You can cycle through the downtown area of Portage la Prairie by taking No. 1A, or ride around the city on No. 1. Then head east on No. 1 to Manitoba's only large city, Winnipeg (where about half of the population of the entire province resides). You can avoid downtown traffic by riding around the city on No. 100, or you can take the well-marked but busy downtown route, which covers about 35 km (20 mi.).

Winnipeg has many attractions, including the Legislative Building, the Manitoba Museum of Man and Nature, the Manitoba Planetarium, the Western Canada Aviation Museum, the Ukrainian Cultural and Educational Centre, the Royal Canadian Mint, and the Assiniboine Park Zoo.

After your visit to Winnipeg, continue on the Trans Canada Highway (No. 1). Just east of Winnipeg is a sign telling you that you have now reached the longitudinal center of Canada. You can continue across the province and into Ontario on No. 1 (described in Alternate Section No. 1, previously), but I recommend cycling south on No. 12 to Ste. Anne and Steinbach.

You will pass signs that urge you to "Buy Your Next Car in Steinbach," as it is considered to be the automobile city of Manitoba with several prosperous automobile dealerships. Steinbach is also the site of Mennonite Heritage Village, which depicts Mennonite life in the 1800s. Delicious Dutch food is yet another feature of this dry town (no alcohol outlets).

The flat terrain continues as you cycle south through southern Manitoba on No. 12. You ride through a rather sparsely populated area as you travel to Zhoda, South Junction, and Sprague. You then cross the border into the United States.

Minnesota

450 km (270 mi.)

Take No. 313 to Warroad, Minnesota, located on the southwest tip of Lake of the Woods (part of this lake is in Canada and part of it is in the United States). Warroad is sometimes referred to as Hockeytown, U.S.A. It is known for its hockey sticks, its walleye, and its location as the second largest window manufacturer in the United States, Marvin Windows (tours are available).

Cycle southwest on No. 11 from Warroad to Baudette, which claims to be the walleye capital of the world and to have the best fishing anywhere. From Baudette, you can continue on No. 11 to International Falls; however, a shorter route to this destination is to cross the border back into Canada at Rainy River, Ontario. Continue east on No. 11, where the road is rather bumpy, with no paved shoulder; however, the traffic is light and the terrain is relatively flat (although there are some hills in the Emo area). Ride through Emo to Fort Frances,

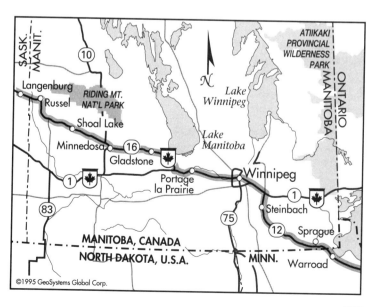

©1995 GeoSystems Global Corp.

then cross the border back into the United States at International Falls, Minnesota.

A large statue of Smokey the Bear and a giant thermometer are located at International Falls, which claims to be the icebox of the nation because of its low temperatures. Voyageurs National Park is near International Falls.

Minnesota has over 300 km (180 mi.) of off-road bicycle trails, 3,500 km (2,100 mi.) of snowmobile trails, 850 km (500 mi.) of horseback riding trails, and nearly 2,500 km (1,500 mi.) of state hiking trails.

Head south from International Falls on No. 53, through Kabetogama State Forest and Superior National Forest. This is an excellent road for cycling, with its wide paved shoulder—you will feel as if you have an entire lane to yourself. As you cycle through scenic, forested northern Minnesota, you are very apt to see a number of deer; however, you may also see several lumber trucks on this route.

Ride to Orr, Cook, Virginia, Eveleth (home of the U.S. Hockey Hall of Fame), Cotton, and Duluth. You travel on a 4-lane highway from Virginia to Duluth.

Duluth has the Lake Superior Zoological Garden, a busy harbor (ships of 35 foreign nations visit this port each year), and Lake Superior Paper Industries (public tours available). The Bayfront Blues Festival is held in Duluth annually.

At Duluth, visit the Enger Memorial Tower on Skyline Parkway (at the highest point of land in Duluth). This is an excellent spot from which to view the Duluth-Superior harbor area before descending (on a 9% grade) and crossing from Duluth, Minnesota, to Superior, Wisconsin.

Take note that you must leave No. 53 at Duluth. Do not cross the Blatnik Bridge (on No. 53), as it is far too dangerous for bicycles; instead, go over to No. 2 in Duluth and then cross by way of this bridge into Superior, Wisconsin. There is heavy traffic in the Duluth-Superior area.

Wisconsin

184 km (110 mi.)

Superior, Wisconsin, offers ship tours of the S.S. Meteor, the last remaining whaleback ship, built in 1896.

The shoulder of the road is narrow, but good, as you leave Superior and cycle east on No. 2, through Brule River State Forest and Chequamegon National Forest, to Wentworth, Iron River (home of Blueberry Festival Days), and Ashland.

The Apostle Islands are located near Ashland. For an interesting side trip, you might like to explore this area. The largest of the Apostle Islands is Madeline Island, which is 23 km (14 mi.) long; it contains 75 km (45 mi.) of roads for cyclists. A short ferry ride will take you from Bayfield to Madeline Island.

Continue cycling east on No. 2 from Ashland to Odanah, on the Bad River Indian Reservation, and Hurley, near the Michigan border. You will notice many Bear Crossing and Deer Crossing signs on this route across the northern section of the state of Wisconsin, near the southern shore of Lake Superior. The state of Wisconsin has almost 9,000 lakes, and you ride past several of them on this route. You may also sight bald eagles as you ride along.

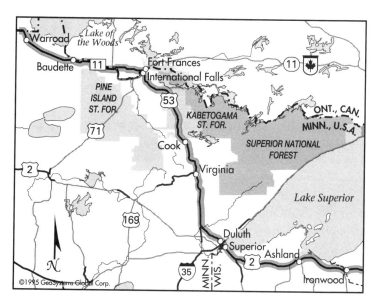

Michigan

18 km (311 mi.)

Cross the border from Wisconsin into Michigan, and continue on No. 2 to Ironwood, site of the large statue of Hiawatha. Near Ironwood is Copper Peak, where you can take a chairlift for a view of Minnesota, Wisconsin, Michigan, Lake Superior, and Thunder Bay, Ontario.

Cycle from Ironwood to Wakefield, a ski resort. Then ride northeast on No. 28 to Bergland, on Lake Gogebic, in the vicinity of the last U.S. stagecoach holdup, for which Black Bart served 24 years. Continue on No. 28 to Bruce Crossing; Trout Creek; Covington; Michigamme, where *Anatomy of a Murder* was filmed in a house that is now a restaurant; Champion; Ishpeming, the location of the U.S. National Ski Hall of Fame and a gift shop called The Tourist Trap; Negaunee, with the Iron Industry Museum; and Marquette, a principal shipping port of iron ore and the site of the Olympic Education Center.

The traffic is heavier in the Marquette area; there is a bike path through the city for your convenience and safety.

The section of No. 28 from Marquette to Munising (about 50 km/30 mi.) is particularly scenic; you cycle along the shore of Lake Superior. There are several picturesque stops along this route, including several sandy beaches. You will cycle through the village of Christmas, where Christmas cards, gifts, and decorations are on display all year.

At Munising, there is an underwater preserve where you can scuba dive and view the shipwrecks that are preserved in the clear waters of Munising Bay. You can take a scenic route from Munising, along the Pictured Rocks National Lakeshore, or a boat cruise of these picturesque rock formations, which were described in Longfellow's poem *Song of Hiawatha*.

From Munising, continue east on No. 28 through Hiawatha National Forest and Lake Superior State Park. Ride through Wetmore to Shingleton (where the Iverson Snowshoe Company makes snowshoes out of ash trees) and Seney. The 96,000-acre Seney National Wildlife Refuge, the largest wildlife refuge in the United States east of the Mississippi River, is located at Seney, and it is a stopover for many migratory birds. Parts of this refuge are accessible only by canoe. Mountain bikes can be rented in the refuge; 135 km (80 mi.) of trails are available.

The terrain is very flat as you cycle from Wetmore to Seney, but it becomes hilly in the Newberry area. Newberry is best known as the gateway to Tahquamenon Falls, Michigan's largest falls; there is a Lower Falls and a more spectacular Upper Falls, 7 km (4 mi.) apart. If you want to take a side trip from Newberry to visit Tahquamenon Falls, head north on No. 123. You can also continue to Paradise and Whitefish Point (site of the Great Lakes Shipwreck Historical Museum, which features the ore carrier *Edmund Fitzgerald*; it sank in a November gale and was remembered in a song by the Canadian singer Gordon Lightfoot); however, this side trip would add about 170 km (100 mi.) to your journey.

Continue east on No. 28 from Newberry to the freeway (No. 75); cross the freeway (which is off-limits to cyclists), and ride north on No. 129 to Sault Ste. Marie, Michigan's oldest community.

The Ojibway Indians used to portage around the rapids on the St. Mary's River. A passage around the rapids was created by the Soo Locks, which raise and lower ocean vessels and Great Lakes ore freighters between Lake Superior and the St. Mary's River at Sault Ste. Marie. There is a visitor's viewing

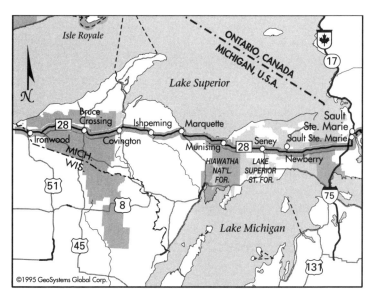

area from which to watch the freighters go through the locks. You can also get a panoramic view from the Tower of History and from the International Bridge.

Ontario

1,175 km (705 mi.)

You will pay a small fee to cross the International Bridge from Sault Ste. Marie, Michigan, to Sault Ste. Marie, Ontario. This Ontario city holds one of the largest Winter Carnivals (Bon Soo) in Canada. Sault Ste. Marie, Ontario, is also the site of such points of interest as the Art Gallery of Algoma, the Great Lakes Forest Research Centre, Ermatinger House (Canada's oldest stone house west of Toronto), Heritage Village, and the Sault Museum. The M.S. *Norgami* is on display; it was the last passenger cruise ship built on the Great Lakes; it ran from Owen Sound to the Sault and, later, served as a ferry between Manitoulin Island and the Bruce Peninsula. If you wish, you can take a 190 km (114 mi.) journey by train into Agawa Canyon, which is particularly picturesque in the autumn.

Leave Sault Ste. Marie, on the Trans Canada Highway; follow it (No. 17) to Garden River (on an Ojibway Indian Reservation), Bruce Mines, Thessalon, Iron Bridge, the Mississagi Chutes (on the Mississagi River), and Blind River. There is a narrow paved shoulder for most of this route as you ride along the north shore of the North Channel of Lake Huron.

Continue to cycle on the busy Trans Canada Highway from Blind River to Serpent River (where there is a scenic waterfall near the highway of this largely French-speaking community), Spanish, and Massey (which hosts the Voyageur Marathon each summer). You can continue east on No. 17 to Sudbury, but I recommend turning south on No. 6 to Espanola, where you cross the Spanish River. The Espanola area offers fishing, hunting (for duck, deer, bear, and moose), camping, canoeing, horseback riding, snowmobiling, and birdwatching. E. B. Eddy Forest Products gives tours of its forest operations and mill.

It is about 135 km (80 mi.) across Manitoulin Island from Espanola to the ferry dock at South Baymouth. There is no paved shoulder for most of this route, but the traffic should be relatively light. Watch for several species of birds as you cycle along, including loons, hummingbirds, cranes, ravens, hawks, and turkey vultures. You face some difficult climbs as you cycle through the La Cloche Mountains; the climbs are particularly tough between Espanola and Birch Island, and there is a long climb from Sheguiandah to Ten Mile Point, where you will find a scenic outlook.

Head south on No. 6 from Espanola to Whitefish Falls; Birch Island; Little Current, where there is a one-lane bridge that swings open for boats—watch the lights here; Sheguiandah; Manitowaning; and South Baymouth, where you pay a fee to board a ferry for a nearly 2-hour ride to Tobermory at the tip of the Bruce Peninsula.

Tobermory attracts many tourists. The cairn for the famous Bruce Trail, a 750 km (450 mi.) hiking trail from Tobermory to Queenston Heights near Niagara Falls, is located at Tobermory. The section of the trail on the Bruce Peninsula offers spectacular views of Georgian Bay. Tobermory is known both as the orchid capital and the underwater capital of Canada. Fathom Five National Marine Park, Canada's first national marine park, is located here; there are more than 20 historic shipwrecks for divers to explore. Bruce Peninsula National Park is also found near Tobermory.

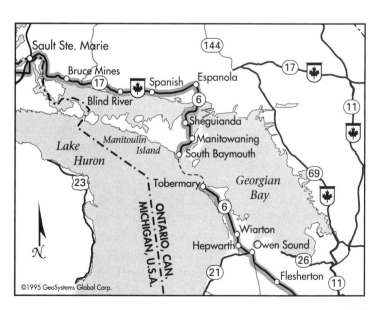

There is no paved shoulder on No. 6 as you cycle south from Tobermory to Miller Lake, Clarke's Corners, Ferndale, and Wiarton, which is considered to be the groundhog capital of Canada. Wiarton is the home of Wiarton Willie, a white albino groundhog that forecasts, on February 2, when spring will arrive.

The Bruce Peninsula has over 850 km (500 mi.) of majestic shoreline. There are spectacular views from cliffs overlooking Georgian Bay, and there are scenic caves to be explored (the movie *Quest For Fire* was filmed in this area). Another park, Sauble Falls Provincial Park, is also on this peninsula.

Continue cycling from Wiarton to Hepworth on No. 6. Then take No. 70 to Shallow Lake and No. 6 to Owen Sound. You cross the 45th parallel, midway between the North Pole and the Equator, as you ride.

There is a tough climb at Owen Sound as you continue on No. 6 south to Chatsworth. Then turn southeast on No. 10, and ride to Markdale, Flesherton, and Shelburne. Nicknamed Fiddletown, Shelburne hosts the Canadian Old Time Fiddle Championships.

From Shelburne, travel northeast on No. 89 to Primrose. Turn south on No. 10 to Orangeville. Then cycle northeast on No. 9 to Newmarket. This route is rather hilly, but the traffic is relatively light (considering the proximity to Toronto). As you approach Newmarket, notice the black, rich soil; you are near the Holland Marsh area, which has some of the best vegetable-growing land in North America. Several excellent vegetable markets are found in this vicinity.

Ride northeast on No. 31 from Newmarket. Then take No. 8 to Uxbridge (with its Quaker heritage) and Port Perry. Continue east on No. 7A to Blackstock. Then head south on No. 57, a quiet country road with some nice descents to Bowmanville.

This route from Owen Sound to Bowmanville changes roads quite often, to spend most of the time on less-traveled, safer country roads, but you meet No. 2 at Bowmanville and cycle on it for much of your trip through southeastern Ontario.

Follow along the shore of Lake Ontario as you cycle on No. 2 from Bowmanville to Port Hope, where there is quite a descent on the main street; Cobourg; Colborne; and Brighton, where there is an interesting side-trip to Presqu'ile Provincial Park. Continue east to Trenton, with its large air force base, and Belleville, the "friendly city". You may like to take a side trip here by cycling across the bridge into Prince Edward County and riding to the beautiful sand dunes at Sandbanks Provincial Park, described in Chapter 10.

Continue on No. 2 from Belleville to Napanee, Kingston (where Old Fort Henry is located), and Gananoque. At Gananoque you can take a scenic boat tour of the Thousand Islands area.

You can continue east on No. 2 from Gananoque, but I recommend taking the scenic Thousand Islands Bikeway, an excellent 35 km (20 mi.) bike path. You ride from Gananoque to Ivy Lea, Rockport, and Mallorytown (headquarters of St. Lawrence Islands National Park).

Rejoin No. 2 after riding on the bike path, and travel east to Brockville, Prescott, and Morrisburg. Near Morrisburg is Upper Canada Village, a re-created 19th-century pioneer village, which includes such facilities as a blacksmith shop, a general store, and a sawmill.

Cycling through the St. Lawrence Seaway Valley, which is a relatively flat area. As you approach the southeastern Ontario city of Cornwall, there is an excellent paved bike path for about the last 20 km (12 mi.); the bike path has washroom

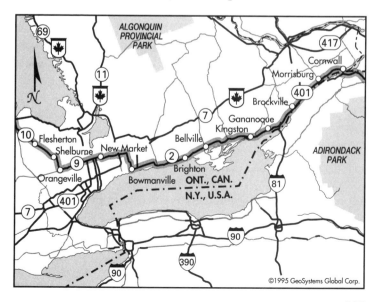

facilities, rest areas, wooded areas, and parkland with picnic tables. The path avoids the traffic of downtown Cornwall and leads you to the Seaway International Bridge.

New York

150 km (90 mi.)

As you leave Ontario and cross the Seaway International Bridge into New York State, take note that the American span of the bridge has large expansion joints that are very dangerous for bicycles; walk your bike over these joints.

Follow No. 11 east through the foothills of the Adirondacks to the Vermont state line. This route has a wide paved shoulder. Cycle through Rooseveltown, Fort Covington, Chateaugay, Mooers, and Champlain. An interesting side trip is to take No. 374, No. 3, and No. 86 to drink in the beauty of the White Face Mountains area, including the towns of Saranac Lake and Lake Placid.

Vermont

240 km (144 mi.)

At Rouses Point, cross the bridge over Lake Champlain (the largest body of fresh water east of the Great Lakes) from New York to Vermont. Proceed to Swanton, and take No. 78 east to Enosburg Falls. Then go south on No. 108 to Bakersfield and Jeffersonville, and southeast on No. 15 to Morrisville. You are now near many popular Vermont skiing areas, including Smugglers Notch and Stowe. Many trails in these mountains are shared by skiers, hikers, and equestrians. Stowe has an excellent bike path from the village to the ski area. A short side trip takes you to Waterbury, the site of Ben and Jerry's famous ice cream plant.

Vermont is a popular, if challenging, biking area. You encounter some steep climbs and many picturesque spots as you cycle through the Green Mountains. In fact, your toughest climbs come on No. 15 as you ride from Hardwick to Walden; this is also an excellent area for spotting black bear.

Continue cycling on No. 15 until you meet No. 2. Then head east on No. 2 to St. Johnsbury, where you experience the ecstasy of a nice, long descent into the town. Ride on to North Concord, Lunenburg, and the New Hampshire state line.

New Hampshire

65 km (39 mi.)

Crossing the state line from Vermont to New Hampshire, stay on No. 2 through the White Mountains, which cross the state from southwest to northeast. Cycle on No. 2 to Lancaster and Jefferson.

This is a very picturesque area for cycling. You view the Presidential range in the White Mountains as you continue east to Randolph and descend into the Mount Washington Valley at Gorham (in the heart of the White Mountains National Forest and close to the Appalachian Trail and the Great Gulf Wilderness area). From Gorham, continue to the state border.

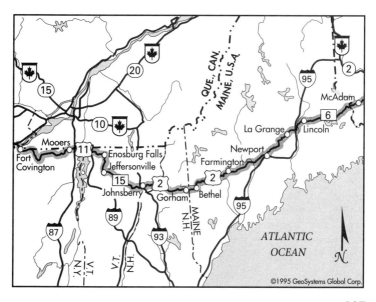

Maine

395 km (237 mi.)

Continue on No. 2 as you cycle from New Hampshire to Maine and arrive at Gilead, Bethel, Rumford, Farmington, Skowhegan, and Newport. You will see several potato fields and Moose Crossing signs along this route; the traffic is relatively light, and there is a narrow paved shoulder much of the way. However, you face the challenge of yet another mountain range (the Longfellow Mountains) as you cycle through northern Maine. At Newport, head northwest on No. 11 (the Moosehead Route) to East Corinth. Then take No. 43 and No. 221 to Bradford. Take No. 155 to Lagrange, and then cycle on No. 6 to Howland and Lincoln. This area is rather desolate, so be sure to carry some supplies.

As you continue your journey on No. 6, be prepared for some tough climbs, particularly on the 35 km (20 mi.) stretch from Springfield to Topsfield. You will be riding through vast forests—I saw a black bear once right on the road. You are cycling on the International Lakeland Trail, which goes from Lincoln, Maine, to Fredericton, New Brunswick.

New Brunswick

360 km (216 mi.)

Cross from St. Croix, Maine, to McAdam, New Brunswick, as you once again return to Canada. There will not be a great feeling of relief as you descend out of the mountains, for the terrain remains hilly all the way to Fredericton. Ride northeast in the Lower St. John Valley on No. 4 from McAdam to Harvey. Take No. 3 and then No. 2 (the Trans Canada Highway) to Fredericton.

Fredericton, named in honor of the second son of King George III, was once an important military center; traces of this era are still evident at Officer's Square and Compound. Other points of interest in the Fredericton area include Christ Church Cathedral (consecrated in 1853), Odell Park, the National Exhibition Centre, the Provincial Sports Hall of Fame, and the New Brunswick Craft School (the only post-secondary institute of its kind in Canada). The World Town Crier Championships are held in Fredericton each summer.

Remain on the Trans Canada Highway from Fredericton to Youngs Cove Road, cycling through a very flat section along the St. John River (from Fredericton to Jemseg). The highway is very busy, but there is a wide paved shoulder.

Travel northeast on No. 112 to Moncton. This road is much quieter—and it's a shortcut. At Moncton, you can visit Magnetic Hill, a gravity-defying phenomenon where cars appear to coast uphill. You might also be interested in Bore Park, where the relentless tides of the Bay of Fundy raise water levels a great amount in just over an hour (this occurs twice daily). A worthwhile side trip would be to visit Fundy National Park and the Hopewell Cape area, where you can walk amid the flowerpot rocks at low tide. This side trip is described in Chapter 7, as one of the recommended tours.

From Moncton, travel east on No. 2 and then on No. 15 to Shediac, called the lobster capital of the world. Many of the town's restaurants specialize in seafood. As you cycle into Shediac, you will be greeted by a large statue of a lobster.

Continue southeast on No. 15 through Cap-Pele (a French-speaking area), and then take No. 955 from Shemogue to Cape Tormentine. This route is very quiet and takes you along the coast to the ferry dock at Cape Tormentine.

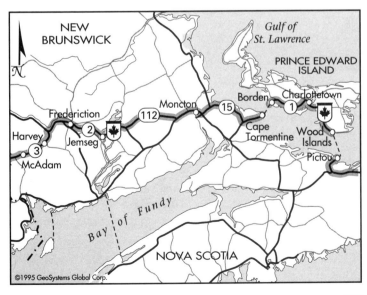

Prince Edward Island

120 km (72 mi.)

Take the toll ferry from Cape Tormentine, New Brunswick, to Borden, on Prince Edward Island. Notice the red soil, due to the presence of iron oxide, as you begin cycling on Prince Edward Island, a province famous for its seafood, potatoes, fishing, lady slippers, and Irish heritage.

Prince Edward Island is known as the Garden of the Gulf. The Micmac Indians called it Abegweit, "the home cradled on the waves." Canada's smallest province has the most kilometers of paved roads per capita in the country. Several scenic routes are posted by the Department of Tourism.

Your route through Prince Edward Island is quite flat and has a paved shoulder. From Borden, take No. 1 to Cape Traverse (where a replica of one of the old iceboats is displayed), Crapaud, Bonshaw, Cornwall, and Charlottetown, Canada's smallest provincial capital. Charlottetown is called the birthplace of Canada because the Fathers of Confederation met here for the first time.

The Trans Canada Highway will take you right through Charlottetown. Then continue east to Orwell, Belfast, Pinette (one of the island's many clam-digging areas), and Wood Islands, where you can take a ferry to Nova Scotia.

Nova Scotia

283 km (170 mi.)

Take the 20 km (12 mi.) ferry ride from Wood Islands, Prince Edward Island, to Caribou, Nova Scotia. Cycle on No. 106 from Caribou to Pictou, where Scottish Highlanders arrived in 1773 and began the wave of Scottish immigration. Pictou is known as the birthplace of New Scotland, and it is the largest community on the Northumberland Strait.

Cycle from Pictou to New Glasgow, which is named after the Scottish hometown of the area's first settler, James Carmichael. The community's Scottish heritage is celebrated here by the Johnny Miles Marathon and the Festival of the Tartans, both annual events.

Ride east on the Trans Canada Highway (now No. 104) from New Glasgow to Antigonish and Auld Cove. Cross the Canso

Causeway (toll bridge), and take No. 105 to Kingsville, Melford, Blue Mills, Nyanza (a Micmac Indian reserve), and Baddeck, where the Alexander Graham Bell National Historic Museum displays many of Bell's inventions. This route is quite busy, but there is a wide paved shoulder most of the way.

Known as Canada's ocean playground, Nova Scotia is almost completely surrounded by water: the Bay of Fundy, Northumberland Strait, the Gulf of St. Lawrence, and the Atlantic Ocean. No part of Nova Scotia is more than 60 km (35 mi.) from a large body of water.

Complete your route through Nova Scotia by cycling on No. 105 from Baddeck to North Sydney's ferry dock, about 100 km (95 mi.) from the Canso Causeway (the world's deepest). You can take a 165 km (100 mi.) ride to Channel-Port-aux-Basques, Newfoundland, or a 443 km (266 mi.) ride to Argenti, Newfoundland (advance reservations are required).

Newfoundland

910 km (546 mi.) from Channel-Port-aux-Basques or 140 km (84 mi.) from Argentia

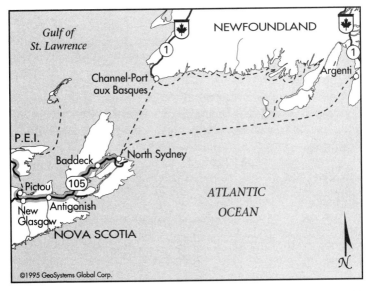

Newfoundland is a rugged island in the Atlantic Ocean. Most of the population resides in coastal fishing settlements. It is one of the oldest settled regions in North America, but it is also Canada's youngest province (becoming part of Canada on March 31, 1949). Newfoundland is famous for its excellent hunting and fishing; moose, caribou, and black bear are in abundance, as are lobster, salmon, trout, and cod.

Your route across Newfoundland is sparsely populated, so be prepared; careful planning is required, particularly if you are not camping along the way.

If you plan to cycle across the province, begin at Channel-Port-aux-Basques and ride on No. 1 to John Cheeseman Provincial Park (with a sandy beach), Mummichog Provincial Park (offering 15 km/9 mi. of beach—and a good place for birdwatching), and Corner Brook. Located at the mouth of the Humber River, which is known for its salmon, Corner Brook is Newfoundland's second largest city. Corner Brook hosts the Hangashore Folk Festival each summer, showcasing traditional performers from throughout the province.

The terrain becomes more hilly after you leave Corner Brook, and there are some especially tough climbs between South Brook and Deer Lake as you cycle through the Long Range Mountains. Continue on No. 1 to Windsor, Bishops Falls, Gander, and Terra Nova Provincial Park.

Terra Nova Provincial Park includes deeply indented coastline, rocky fjords, and inland ponds. Icebergs, whales, and seals can often be seen off the coast of this park, Canada's easternmost provincial park.

Complete your trip by cycling through the park and continuing your ride to St. John's, the capital city of Newfoundland and the closest North American city to Europe. St. John's has retained many historic buildings and sites to preserve its past. The annual St. John's Regatta is considered the oldest organized sports event in North America.

If, instead of the previously described route, you take the ferry from Sydney, Nova Scotia, to Argentia, Newfoundland, cycle on No. 100 and No. 1 (the Trans Canada Highway) to St. John's, your destination.

Alternate Routes

Alternate Route 1: Manitoba, Ontario

In Manitoba, remain on the Trans Canada Highway (No. 1) out of Winnipeg and, instead of cycling south to the border, continue east on No. 1 into Ontario (where the Trans Canada Highway becomes No. 17). Ride to Thunder Bay, and then follow the rugged north shore of Lake Superior to Sault Ste. Marie where you rejoin the main route.

This section of northern Ontario is very hilly and has fewer services than in the south. The route is challenging and has a lot of truck and tourist traffic. However, there are spectacular views of the rugged coastline of Lake Superior.

Alternate Route 2. Ontario

If you follow my suggested route through southern Ontario, but decide to stay in Canada rather than cross into New York State, continue east on No. 2 at Cornwall, Ontario. Cross the bridge on No. 201, past Coteau Landing, and remain on No. 201 until you join No. 202 in southern Quebec. Cycle east on No. 202 to Cowansville. Ride northeast on No. 241 to Warden, No. 220 to Ste.-Anne-de-la- Rochelle, and No. 243 to Racine. Take No. 222 and No. 249 to Windsor.

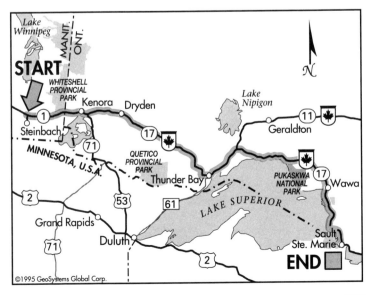

©1995 GeoSystems Global Corp.

Continue cycling northeast on No. 249 from Windsor to
St.-Georges-de-Windsor. Ride northeast to Wottonville, and
then take No. 216 to St.-Adrien, St.-Julien, and St.-Ferdinand
(on Lac William). Cycle northwest on No. 265 all the way to
the St. Lawrence River at Deschaillons. Follow the St.
Lawrence River as you ride northeast on No. 132 through
Quebec City and on to Rivière-du-Loup.

This route through Quebec takes you on quieter roads, most
without a paved shoulder. Most of the trip is on paved roads,
but there are some gravel sections on No. 216.

Cycle southeast on No. 185 from Rivière-du-Loup to New
Brunswick, and then take the Trans Canada Highway (No. 2),
with a wide paved shoulder and heavy traffic, all the way to
Fredericton, New Brunswick. Here you will rejoin the
detailed, described route.

This route includes several hilly sections, particularly in the
Eastern Townships, as you cycle across Quebec.

Alternate Route 3: Quebec

If you decide to ride across Canada by way of the province of
Quebec, there is a more direct route—by changing your
Ontario route much earlier. At Espanola in northern Ontario,
do not turn south; instead, continue cycling on the busy

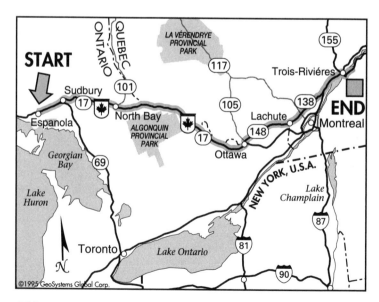

Trans Canada Highway (No. 17) to Sudbury, North Bay, and Pembroke. Then cross the Ottawa River into Quebec and cycle south on No. 148 to the Hull/Ottawa area.

Although this is a route taken by some, I do not recommend it, because the route across Manitoulin Island is much safer. However, if you do decide on this very busy alternate route, take care. You will find that the narrow paved shoulder will disappear after Espanola, making the road more dangerous for the cyclist.

You will also find sections of No. 17 off-limits to the cyclist through the cities, so that alternate routes have to be found (such as No. 55 near Sudbury). The heavy traffic, off-limits sections, and inconsistent paved shoulder makes the route in Alternate Section No. 2 much better. However, if you do decide on this route, you will cross into the province of Quebec from Ottawa, Ontario, and then cycle east on No. 148 to Lachute. Then ride northeast on No. 158 and No. 138 to Trois-Rivières. Cross the river, and then cycle northeast on No. 132, where you will soon meet up with the route through Quebec described in Alternate Section No. 2. Follow the route previously suggested until you again rejoin the detailed route from coast to coast (at Fredericton, New Brunswick).

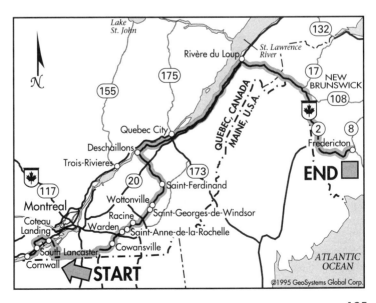

Appendix

1. Addresses

Canada Customs
269 Main St.
Winnipeg, Manitoba R3C 1B3
Telephone (204) 983-6004

Canadian Cycling Assoc.
1600 Naismith Drive, Suite 810
Gloucester, Ontario K1B 5N4
Telephone (613) 748-5629

Canadian Hostelling
Association
1600 Naismith Drive, Suite 608
Gloucester, Ontario K1B 5N4
Telephone (613) 748-5638

2. Hotlines for Tourist Information

For free provincial maps and guides that cover activities, festivals, events, attractions, accommodations, eating, and camping, phone the following hotlines:

Alberta: 1-800-661-8888
British Columbia: 1-800-663-6000
Manitoba: 1-800-665-0040
New Brunswick: 1-800-561-0123
Newfoundland: 1-800-563-6353

Northwest Territories: 1-800-661-0788
Nova Scotia: 1-800-565-0000
Ontario: 1-800-668-2746 (English); 1-800-268-3736 (French)
Prince Edward Island: 1-800-565-0267
Quebec: 1-800-363-7777

Saskatchewan: 1-800-667-7191
Yukon: 1-800-661-0494

3. Bicycle Touring Companies

This list is not complete, but here are several commercial bicycle tour operators who offer organized tours in Canada:

Adventure Cycling
Association
P.O. Box 8308
Missoula, MT 59807-8308
Telephone (406) 721-1776

Alberta Alpine Adventures
Box 2, Suite 38
R.R. No. 12
Calgary, Alberta T3E 6W3
Telephone (403) 288-8612

Avalon Bicycle Tours
P.O. Box 925
St. John's, Newfoundland,
A1C 5L7
Telephone (709) 576-1951

Backroads
1516 - 5th St. Suite Q333
Berkeley, CA 94710-1740
Telephone 1-800-245-3874
(510) 527-1555
FAX (510) 527-1444

Bicycle Ontario Tours
P.O. Box 20044
North Bay, Ontario P1B 9N1
Telephone (705) 752-5693

Butterfield and Robinson
70 Bond St.
Toronto, Ontario M5B 1X3
Telephone (416) 864-1354

Canadian Back Routes
597 Markham St.
Toronto, Ontario M6G 2L7
Telephone (416) 588-6137

Canadian Trails Bicycle Tours
R.R. No.2
Chatham Ontario N7M 5J7
Telephone 1-800-668-2453

Canuso Cycle Tours
9932 Maplecreek Dr. SE
Calgary, Alberta T2J 1T6

Countryroads Bike Tours
P.O. Box 70657
2938 Dundas St. W
Toronto, Ontario M6P 4E7

Covered Bridge Bicycle Tours
P.O. Box 693
Main Post Office
St. John, N.B. E2L 4B3

Cycleventures Ltd.
R.R. No. 2
2517 Wilhaven Dr.
Cumberland, Ontario K0A 1S0
Telephone (613) 833-3343

Down East Tours
Comp. 41K
R.R. No. 2
Kingston, N.S. B0P 1R0
Telephone (902) 765-8923

Freewheeling Adventures Inc.
R.R. No. 1
Hubbards, N.S. B0J 1G0
Telephone (902) 857-3600
FAX (902) 857-3612

Fresh Tracks
1823 West Fourth Ave.
Vancouver, B.C. V6J 1M4

Gabriola Island Cycle and
Kayak
9775 - 5th St.
Sydney, B.C. V8L 2X1
Telephone (604) 656-9888

Galiano Guided Bicycle
Tours
R.R. No. 1
Galiano Island, B.C. V0N 1P0
Telephone (604) 539-2806

Georgian Shores Cycle Tours
688 - 8th St. A East
Owen Sound, Ontario
N4K 1N2
Telephone (519) 371-7889

Grand Bicycle Tours
Box 37 Site 2
R.R. No. 1
Elora, Ontario N0B 1S0
Telephone (519) 846-8455

Great Canadian Bicycle Tours
P.O. Box 245
Paris, Ontario N3L 3G2

Kootenay Mountain Bike
Tours
Box 867
Nelson, B.C. V1L 6A5
Telephone (604) 354-4371

MacQueen's Bike Shop and
Travel Agency
430 Queen St.
Charlottetown, P.E.I. C1A 4E8
Telephone/FAX
(902) 368-2453

Okanagan Bike Roads
939 Dynes Ave.
Penticton, B.C. V2A 1E7
Telephone (604) 493-2453

Receptour International
555 boule. Rene-Levesque W.
Montreal, Quebec H2Z 1B1
Telephone (514) 871-9637

Rent-A-Bike/Cycle Tour
P.O. Box 1204, Sta. B
Ottawa, Ontario K1P 5P3
Telephone (613) 233-0268

Rocky Mountain Cycle Tour
L Barnes
Box 1978
Canmore, Alberta T0L 0M0
Telephone 1-800-661-2453

Singing Sands Sea Breeze
Nature Trails Kingsboro
R.R. No. 2
Souris, P.E.I. C0A 2B0
Telephone (902) 357-2371
1-800-667-2371

Singles Bicycle Tours Inc.
550 First St.
Collingwood, Ontario L9Y 1C1
Telephone (705) 444-2813

Spinning Wheel Bicycle
Tours Box 51
Jordan Station, Ontario L0R 1S0
Telephone (416) 562-7169

Sunset Bicycle Tours
455 University Ave.
Charlottetown, P.E.I. C1A 4N8
Telephone (902) 892-0606

Timberline Bicycle Tours
7975 E. Harvard Suite J
Denver, CO 80231
Telephone (303) 759-3804

Western Canadian Travel
Consultants
Box 96
Red Deer, Alberta
Telephone (403) 340-0292

Bibliography

The Alberta Bicycle Vacation Guide. Obelisk Enterprise Inc.

Baird, D. M. *A Guide to Geology for Visitors to Canada's National Parks*. Toronto: Macmillan of Canada, 1974.

Canada: A Portrait. 1989. Available from Statistics Canada, Publication Sales and Services, Ottawa, Ont.; phone 1-800-267-6677, (613) 951-7277.

Canadian Book of the Road The Reader's Digest Association (Canada), 1991.

Cayo, D. "Cycling the St. John River Valley," *Canadian Cyclist*. July/August, 1991.

Creighton, D. *Canada: The Heroic Beginnings*. Toronto: Macmillan of Canada, 1974.

The Cyclists' Yellow Pages. Adventure Cycling Association.

Explore Canada. The Reader's Digest Association (Canada) Ltd. (in conjunction with the Canadian Automobile Association), 1974.

Frankton, C., and Mulligan, G. A. *Weeds of Canada*. Toronto: NC Press, 1987.

Gindling, D. "Bordering on the Incredible: 5 Spectacular Canadian Tours," *Bicycling*. July, 1990.

Godfrey, W. E. *The Birds of Canada*. Canada: National Museum of Canada, 1986.

Hall, T. *Wildlife of Canada*. North Vancouver: Whitecap Books, 1987.

Helgason, G., and Dodd, J. *The Canadian Rockies Bicycle Guide*. Lone Pine Publishing, 1986.

Hosie, R. C. *Native Trees of Canada*. Don Mills: Fitzhenry & Whiteside, 1979.

Humber, C. J., ed. *Canada: From Sea Unto Sea*. Mississauga: Heirloom Publishing, 1988.

———. *Canada's Native Peoples*. Mississauga: Heirloom Publishing, 1988.

Katz, E. *The Complete Guide to Bicycling in Canada* (rev. ed.). Toronto: Doubleday Canada Limited, 1989.

Livingston, J. A. *Canada*. Toronto: NSL Natural Science of Canada, 1970.

———. *Canada: The Wonders of Nature*. Toronto: NSL Natural Science of Canada, 1979.

Long-Distance Cycling. Editors of *Bicycling* magazine. Emmaus, Pennsylvania: Rodale Press, 1993.

Lydiard, T. *The British Columbia Bicycling Guide*. Burnaby: Lifestyle Resources, 1984.

Mika, N., and Mika, H. *Prince Edward County Heritage*.

Belleville: Mika Publishing, 1980.

———. *The Settlement of Prince Edward County*. Belleville: Mika Publishing, 1984.

Milne, L., and Milne, M. *The Audubon Society Field Guide to North American Insects and Spiders*. New York: Alfred A. Knopf, 1980.

Nader, R. *Canada First*. Toronto: McClelland & Stewar, 1992.

Pedal Magazine. "Canadian Cycling News. "March, 1994.

Phillips, D. *The Climate of Canada*. 1990. Available through the Canadian Government Publishing Centre, Supply and Services Canada, Ottawa, Ont. K1A 0S9.

Thrasher, B. P. *Alaska and the Yukon*. London: Bison Books, 1985.

"Trail Bicycling in National Parks in Alberta and B. C." Canadian Parks Services, Western Regional Office.

Watkins, M., ed. *Canada*. New York: Facts on File, 1993.

Index

Other Titles Available from Bicycle Books

Title	Author	US Price
All Terrain Biking	Jim Zarka	$7.95
The Backroads of Holland	Helen Colijn	$12.95
The Bicycle Commuting Book	Rob van der Plas	$7.95
The Bicycle Fitness Book	Rob van der Plas	$7.95
The Bicycle Repair Book	Rob van der Plas	$9.95
Bicycle Repair Step by Step (color)*	Rob van der Plas	$14.95
Bicycle Technology	Rob van der Plas	$16.95
Bicycle Touring International	Kameel Nasr	$18.95
The Bicycle Touring Manual	Rob van der Plas	$16.95
Bicycling Fuel	Richard Rafoth, M.D.	$9.95
Cycling Canada	John Smith	$12.95
Cycling Europe	Nadine Slavinski	$12.95
Cycling France	Jerry Simpson	$12.95
Cycling Great Britain	Hughes & Cleary	$12.95
Cycling Kenya	Kathleen Bennett	$12.95
Cycling the San Francisco Bay Area	Carol O'Hare	$12.95
Cycling the U.S. Parks	Jim Clark	$12.95
In High Gear (hardcover)	Samuel Abt	$21.95
The High Performance Heart	Maffetone & Mantell	$10.95
Major Taylor (hardcover)	Andrew Ritchie	$19.95
The Mountain Bike Book	Rob van der Plas	$10.95
Mountain Bike Maintenance (color)	Rob van der Plas	$10.95
Mountain Bikes: Maint. & Repair*	Stevenson & Richards	$22.50
Mountain Bike Racing (hardcover)*	Burney & Gould	$22.50
Mountain Biking the National Parks	Jim Clark	$12.95
The New Bike Book	Jim Langley	$4.95
Roadside Bicycle Repair (color)	Rob van der Plas	$7.95
Tour of the Forest Bike Race (color)	H.E. Thomson	$12.95
Cycle History – 4th Intern. Conference Proceedings (hardcover)		$45.00
Cycle History – 5th Intern. Conference Proceedings (hardcover)		$45.00

Buy our books at your local book store or bike shop.

If you have difficulty obtaining our books elsewhere, we will be pleased to supply them by mail, but we must add $2.50 postage and handling (and California Sales Tax if mailed to a California address). Prepayment by check or credit card must be included.

Bicycle Books, Inc.
1282 - 7th Avenue
San Francisco CA 94122
Tel.: (415) 665-8214
FAX: (415) 753-8572

In Britain: Bicycle Books
463 Ashley Road
Poole, Dorset BH14 0AX
Tel.: (01202) 71 53 49
FAX: (01202) 73 61 91

---

* Books marked thus not available from Bicycle Books in the U.K.